T0349017

Flutter App Development

How to Write for iOS and Android at Once

Rap Payne

Apress®

Flutter App Development: How to Write for iOS and Android at Once

Rap Payne
Dallas, TX, USA

ISBN-13 (pbk): 979-8-8688-0484-7   ISBN-13 (electronic): 979-8-8688-0485-4
https://doi.org/10.1007/979-8-8688-0485-4

Copyright © 2024 by Rap Payne

Managing Director, Apress Media LLC: Welmoed Spahr
Acquisitions Editor: Miriam Haidara
Development Editor: James Markham
Coordinating Editor: Jessica Vakili

Distributed to the book trade worldwide by Springer Science+Business Media New York, 233 Spring Street, 6th Floor, New York, NY 10013. Phone 1-800-SPRINGER, fax (201) 348-4505, e-mail orders-ny@springer-sbm.com, or visit www.springeronline.com. Apress Media, LLC is a California LLC and the sole member (owner) is Springer Science + Business Media Finance Inc (SSBM Finance Inc). SSBM Finance Inc is a **Delaware** corporation.

For information on translations, please e-mail booktranslations@springernature.com; for reprint, paperback, or audio rights, please e-mail bookpermissions@springernature.com.

Apress titles may be purchased in bulk for academic, corporate, or promotional use. eBook versions and licenses are also available for most titles. For more information, reference our Print and eBook Bulk Sales web page at http://www.apress.com/bulk-sales.

Any source code or other supplementary material referenced by the author in this book is available to readers on GitHub via the book's product page, located at https://www.apress.com/gp/services/source-code.

If disposing of this product, please recycle the paper

This book is dedicated to the men and women of the Flutter Community. I've never seen a group more devoted to the success of others. You're an inspiration and example to me.

Particular thanks to these members of the community who've helped me with Flutter issues. This Texan owes y'all!

Andrew "Red" Brogdon (Columbus, Ohio), Brian Egan (Montana), Frederik Schweiger (Düsseldorf, Germany), Jeroen "Jay" Meijer (Rotterdam, Netherlands), Jochum van der Ploeg (Zwolle, Netherlands), Martin Rybak (New York), Martin Jeret (Estonia), Nash Ramdial (Trinidad), Nilay Yenner (San Francisco), Norbert Kozsir (Karlsruhe, Germany), Pooja Bhaumik (Bengaluru, India), Randal Schwartz (Portland, Oregon), Raouf Rahiche (Casablanca by way of Algeria), Remi Rousselet (Paris), Rohan Tanaja (Berlin), and Scott Stoll (Cleveland, Ohio).

But especially Simon Lightfoot (London), who we all call "The Flutter Whisperer." He taught me much of what I know about Flutter.

Worldwide Praise for *Flutter App Development: How to Write for iOS and Android at Once*

"Rap has written a great starting guide full of information for those who are new to developing multi-platform apps with Flutter."

—Frederik Schweiger (Düsseldorf, Germany), organizer of the International Flutter Hackathon and creator of the Flutter School

"A great read! This covers everything a beginner might want to know, and more. It explains not only what Flutter is but why it exists works the way it does. It also provides great tips for common pitfalls along the way. Definitely recommended."

—Jeroen "Jay" Meijer (Rotterdam, Netherlands), leader of Flutter Community GitHub

"Rap's book is a great book to get started with Flutter. It covers every important topic to write your very first app but also contains valuable information for more seasoned developers."

—Norbert Kozsir (Karlsruhe, Germany), Flutter Community editor

"As a non-native English speaker, I'm totally impressed by the simplicity of this book and how much I can read and understand without getting bored."

—Raouf Rahiche (Algeria), Flutter speaker, developer, and instructor

"As an early adopter and one of the original members of the Flutter Community, Rap is one of the world's foremost authorities on Flutter. Where documentation is written for Engineers, by Engineers, Rap is a human who (thankfully!) writes in an enjoyable style that can easily be understood by other humans."

—Scott Stoll (Cleveland, Ohio), contributor to the Flutter codebase and cofounder of the Flutter Study Group

Table of Contents

About the Author

Rap Payne started Agile Gadgets LLC, a mobile app development company, in 2003. Through it, Rap is a consultant, trainer, and entrepreneur who has written apps, mentored developers, and taught software development classes for government agencies like the NSA, FBI, US Air Force, Navy, Army, NASA, and Britain's GCHQ and for Fortune 500 companies like Boeing, Walmart, Coca-Cola, Wells Fargo, CVS, Chase, HP, Lockheed Martin, Exxon-Mobil, Lowe's, Nike, USAA, and Raytheon, to name a few.

Rap and Becky have been married for over 30 years. In addition to their five home-educated children, Rap is a spiritual father to many younger men whom he has mentored over the years. Rap is a middle-of-the-pack marathoner, triathlete, and power lifter.

As a professional mentor and trainer, Rap has mastered teaching highly complex ideas in easy-to-understand ways. And as a real-world developer, he understands the need to teach these topics using practical and realistic examples and exercises.

About the Technical Reviewer

Massimo Nardone has more than 22 years of experience in security, web/mobile development, cloud, and IT architecture. His true IT passions are security and Android.

He has been programming and teaching how to program with Android, Perl, PHP, Java, VB, Python, C/C++, and MySQL for more than 20 years.

He holds a Master of Science in Computing Science from the University of Salerno, Italy.

He has worked as a project manager, software engineer, research engineer, chief security architect, information security manager, PCI/SCADA auditor, and senior lead IT security/cloud/SCADA architect for many years.

His technical skills include security, Android, cloud, Java, MySQL, Drupal, Cobol, Perl, web/mobile development, MongoDB, D3, Joomla, Couchbase, C/C++, WebGL, Python, Pro Rails, django CMS, Jekyll, Scratch, and so on.

He works as Chief Information Security Officer (CISO) for Cargotec Oyj.

He worked as a visiting lecturer and supervisor for exercises at the Networking Laboratory of the Helsinki University of Technology (Aalto University). He holds four international patents (PKI, SIP, SAML, and proxy areas).

Who Is This Book For?

If you're a developer with experience in some object-oriented language like Java, C#, C++, or Objective-C and you want to create Android apps, iOS apps, or web apps with Flutter, this book is for you. It is especially important for you if you want to create an app that runs on multiple platforms and if you are new to Flutter.

If you've got some experience already with Flutter, you'll undoubtedly learn something, but we're not expecting that you have any prerequisite knowledge or experience with Flutter. All of our chapters are written with the assumption that everything in Flutter is completely new to you.

If you know anything about iOS development, Android development, or web development, that will certainly help with understanding the topics because there are lots of analogies in them for Flutter. The more you know about those things, the better, especially JavaScript and React. But if you know none of them, don't fret. They're by no means necessary.

Knowledge of the Dart language also will help. There are some unique but very cool Dart features that we consider best practices. We could have "simplified" the code by not using these best practices, but in the long run, that's not doing you any favors. Instead, we go ahead and use them, but we do explain those things in Appendix A, "Dart Language Overview." In there, we give you a cheat sheet with just enough detail to write code, followed by a more in-depth explanation of the features that will be unexpected by developers of other languages. Pay special attention to the section called "Unexpected Things About Dart."

What Is Covered?

This book teaches you how to create fully functioning and feature-rich apps that run on iOS, Android, desktops, and the Web.

1. Hello Flutter – Welcome to Flutter! We're giving you a feel for why you're here. What problems does Flutter solve? Why the boss would choose Flutter vs. some other solution.

2. Developing in Flutter – Flutter's set of tools aren't always straightforward. We explain what each tool does and how to use it. This chapter guides you through the process of write-debug-test-run. We get an understanding of the tooling including installation and maintenance.

3. Everything Is Widgets – Widgets are super important to Flutter since they're the building blocks of every Flutter app. We show why and provide the motivation and how-to to create widgets. Topics include composition, UI as code, widget types, keys, and stateless vs. stateful widgets.

4. Value Widgets – A deep dive into widgets that hold a value, especially user-input fields. Topics include Text, Image, and Icon widgets and how to create forms in Flutter.

5. Responding to Gestures – How to make your program do things in response to user actions like taps, swiping, pinching, and the like. We'll show you the button family and the GestureDetector widget.

6. Navigation and Routing – Navigation is making the app hide one widget and show another in response to user actions. This makes them feel like they're moving from one scene to another. We'll cover stack navigation, tab navigation, and drawer navigation.

7. Managing State – How to get data from one widget to another and how to change that data. We cover how to create StatefulWidgets and design them in the best way.

8. State Management Libraries – An overview of several libraries and a how-to for a super-simple library called Raw State and the most popular one – Riverpod.

9. Making RESTful API Calls with HTTP – How to read from and write to an HTTP API server. This is where we show how to make GET, POST, PUT, DELETE, and PATCH requests.

10. Styling with Themes – This is where we answer all the questions needed to get a real-world app looking good and staying consistent throughout with styles and themes.

11. Laying Out Your Widgets – The beginning of the final section, this chapter introduces the idea of layouts and steps to control layouts and exposes the Flutter layout algorithm.

12. Layout – Positioning Widgets – How to control how widgets are placed side by side and/or above and below.

13. Layout – Fixing Overflows – What to do when you're trying to draw *more than* will fit on a screen.

14. Layout – Filling Extra Space – What to do when you're trying to draw *less than* will fit. What do you do with that extra space to make it look nice?

15. Layout – Fine-Tuning Positioning – How to adjust the last bits using borders, padding, and margins. How to make nonrectangular shapes.

16. Layout – Special Presentation Widgets – Widgets for when a simple layout won't do the trick – slivers, stack, card, positioned, and table.

And we have five appendixes.

A. Dart Language Overview – An easy-to-parse cheat sheet for Dart itself broken into expected features and pleasant surprises.

B. Futures, Async, and Await – Handling asynchronous activities in Flutter.

C. Including Packages in Your Flutter App – How to find and include the wealth of third-party, publicly available, and free packages. Also how to write and publish your own.

D. How to Work with Files – Using libraries. Futures, async, and await. Bundling files with your app. Reading and writing a file. JSON serialization.

E. How to Debug Your Layout – Interpreting what you see in the visual debugger in both VS Code and Android Studio.

What Is Not Covered and Where Can I Find It?

As importantly, you should know what not to expect in the book. We will not give you a primer on the Dart programming language beyond the aforementioned appendix. We simply didn't think it was the best use of your time and wanted to dive right into Flutter. If you feel you need a primer later on, go here: `https://dart.dev/guides/language/language-tour` followed by `https://dart.dev/tutorials`. We chose not to discuss deploying to the app stores. The stores already do a fine job of explaining how to submit an app. That, and the process, changes so frequently that your definitive resource ought to be the stores themselves. You'll find instructions at `https://developer.apple.com/ios/submit/` and here: `https://play.google.com/apps/publish`. And we aren't going to cover certain advanced topics like device-specific development in iOS and Android or adding Flutter to an existing iOS/Android project. These and so many other topics can be found on the Web by searching.

Foreword

The world of mobile development has shifted. Gone are the days of separate codebases for iOS and Android. Developers today crave efficiency, speed, and the power to reach a wider audience with a single codebase. This is where Flutter shines.

As a Google Developer Expert, I've witnessed firsthand the transformative potential of Flutter. Its elegant architecture, combined with a robust widget library, allows developers to create beautiful and high-performance apps with unmatched speed. The magic of hot reload makes experimentation a breeze, drastically reducing development time and accelerating the iterative process.

But don't let the power of Flutter fool you – it's not without its challenges. Learning a new language and navigating a vast ecosystem of tools and libraries can be daunting. This is where this book comes in.

This book provides a comprehensive guide to Flutter, taking you from the very basics of getting started to more advanced topics like state management and API integration. It is meticulously crafted with clear explanations, practical examples, and hands-on exercises that will solidify your understanding and empower you to build amazing apps.

Whether you're a seasoned developer looking to expand your skillset or a curious beginner eager to enter the world of mobile development, this book is your perfect companion. It's a testament to the dedication and expertise of my friend Rap Payne, and I am confident that it will equip you with the knowledge and confidence to become a successful Flutter developer.

So, embrace the future of cross-platform development and dive into the pages of this invaluable resource. Get ready to build beautiful, performant apps with Flutter!

Randal L. Schwartz

May 2024

Preface

Welcome to *Flutter App Development: How to Write for iOS and Android at Once*! If you're familiar with my earlier work, *Beginning App Development with Flutter*, you might recognize some echoes here and there. That's because this book expands on and renews the topics covered in the first, incorporating the core concepts that made it valuable.

However, consider this a brand-new journey into the ever-evolving world of Flutter development. Since the publication of my first book, Flutter has undergone significant advancements, offering exciting new features and improved workflows. This book reflects those changes, providing a comprehensive and up-to-date exploration of the framework.

While some sections may contain familiar content, you'll find a wealth of new material within these pages. In the first book, we tried to cover layouts in one chapter. Big mistake. In this book, we expanded that to *six* chapters. In the first book, we talked about state management libraries but didn't explain how they worked. Thanks to critique by Remi Rousselet, we moved those chapters much sooner and wrote a how-to for his Riverpod library. And thanks to certain of my clients like Disney and the US State Department, I expanded on existing concepts, drilled deeper into specific functionalities, introduced entirely new sections that address the latest developments, and rearranged the flow to make it easier to learn Flutter.

Whether you're an intermediate Flutter developer building on the basics or a newcomer embarking on your first project, this book aims to be your trusted companion. We'll guide you through the intricacies of building beautiful and performant iOS and Android applications with Flutter, equipping you with the knowledge and skills to navigate the ever-evolving landscape.

So, even if you've traveled this path before, get ready to embark on a fresh adventure with *Flutter App Development: How to Write for iOS and Android at Once*!

Rap Payne

September 2024

CHAPTER 1

Hello Flutter

Picture this in your mind's eye. You are the CEO of a new business. Obviously, your mission is to maximize sales while minimizing expenses. "Hmmm," you think. "I can really increase sales if I make our products available on the Web." So you ask your friends how to create a web app and they say …

"You need to hire a web developer. They should know HTML, CSS, JavaScript, and probably some framework like React, Vue, or Angular."

It's expensive but you do it and your gamble pays off. Sales increase markedly. Trying to keep on top of demand, you monitor social media and engage your customers. You hear them say that this web app is great and all but "We'd have been here earlier if you had an app in the App Store." So you talk to your team who, while being experts in the Web, are not iOS developers. They tell you …

"You need to hire an iOS expert. They should know iOS, Swift or Objective-C, Xcode, macOS, and CocoaPods for development."

Your research shows that this person is *even more* specialized and therefore expensive than your web devs. But again, it seems to be the right thing to do, so you bite the bullet and hire them. But even while this app is being developed, you see that the feedback was not isolated to iOS apps, but instead was looking at all mobile devices. And – oh, snap! – 85% of devices worldwide run Android, not iOS. You bury your head in your hands as you ponder whether or not you can afford to ignore 85% of your potential customers. Your advisors tell you …

R. Payne, *Flutter App Development*, https://doi.org/10.1007/979-8-8688-0485-4_1

"You need to hire an Android expert. They should know the Android OS, Gradle, Android SDK, XML, Android Studio, and Java or Kotlin."

"Really?!? Another developer?", you say. "Yes. And one just as expensive as your iOS developer," they respond.

Isn't there one person who can do all three things? Some way to share the code between all those environments? Then you could hire just one person. In fact, they could write the code one time and deploy it to the Web, to the App Store, and to the Google Play Store. One codebase to maintain. One place to make improvements and upgrades. One place to squash bugs.

Ladies and gentlemen, allow me to introduce you to Flutter!

What Is Flutter?

Flutter is a set of tooling that allows us to create beautiful apps that run on iOS, Android, the Web, Windows, MacOS, and Linux desktops.

Flutter is ...

- Free (as in free beer; no cost)

- Open source (that's the other sense of the word "free")

- Backed by and originated at Google

- Being enhanced and maintained by a team of developers at Google and hundreds of non-Google contributors around the globe

- Currently being used by thousands of developers in organizations across the world for production apps

- Fast because it compiles to truly native apps that don't use crutches like WebViews and JavaScript bridges

- Written one place and compiled to a web app for billions of browsers, an iOS app for iPhones and iPads, and an Android app for all of the rest of the phones and tablets out there

Why Flutter?

Google's mission with Flutter is …

To build a better way to develop for mobile

Notice what is *not* in that mission. There's no mention of Android (which is also owned by Google) nor of iOS nor of the Web. Flutter's goal is to create a better way to develop for all devices. In other words, Flutter should be better to create iOS apps than Swift. It should be better to create Android apps than Kotlin. It should be better to create web apps than HTML/JavaScript. And if you get all of those things simultaneously with one codebase, all the better.

The Flutter team has succeeded spectacularly with this mission.

As proof, Eric Seidel offers this example.[1] The Google CRM team used Flutter to build an internal Android app and did it **three times** faster than with their traditional Android toolchain!

Note   Flutter has delivered on their promise to create web apps and desktop apps. But we must note that relatively few people are choosing Flutter for those apps. The real success story of Flutter has been iOS and Android apps. Consider the other platforms icing on the cake, not the main course.

---

[1] `http://bit.ly/eric_seidel_flutter_keynote_video` at the 21:47 mark

But it turns out that Flutter isn't the only game in town for cross-platform. You have other options.

The Other Options

Cross-platform development comes in three general flavors listed in Table 1-1.

Table 1-1. *Cross-platform development categories*

	Some technologies	Cons	Pros
Progressive web apps (PWA)	HTML/CSS, React, Vue, Angular	Not a real app. Runs in a web browser. Not available in app stores. Hard to create a desktop shortcut. Cannot access many of the device's resources like background processing, compass, proximity sensor, Bluetooth, NFC, and more	Easy to write
Hybrid	PhoneGap, Cordova, Sencha, Capacitor, Ionic	Runs in a WebView so it can be slow. Nearly impossible to share code with the web app	Easier for web devs to learn because it uses HTML and JavaScript as its language and structure
Compile-to-native solutions	React Native, NativeScript, Flutter, Maui	Learning a framework may be difficult. Mastering the toolchain definitely is	Real apps that can be found in the stores and run fast

If you have a captive audience, one where users value your app so much that they're willing to accept a poorer user experience, the cheapest solution is to create a PWA. If your app is extremely naive and speed is not expected to be an issue, a hybrid solution might be appropriate. But if speed, smoothness, and sophisticated capability are important, you will need to go with a native solution.

Native Solutions

As of today, there are four fairly popular compile-to-native solutions (Table 1-2).

Table 1-2. *Compile-to-native cross-platform frameworks*

	Maui	**NativeScript**	**React Native**	**Flutter**
Year introduced	2011	2014	2015	2018
Backed by	Microsoft	Telerik	Facebook	Google
Presentation language	XAML and/or xamarin.forms	Proprietary but looks like XML	Proprietary but looks like JSX	Dart
Procedural language	C#	JavaScript	JavaScript	Dart

These are all decent options. All are free to develop in and are well tested, having many production applications created. All have been used in large organizations.

Flutter is the latest of these frameworks to be released. As such, it has a distinct advantage of observing those that had come before. The Flutter team took note of what worked well with other frameworks and what failed. In addition, Flutter added new innovations and ideas – all baked in from the start rather than being bolted on as improvements are made.

But I suspect that if you've bought this book, you don't need much convincing, so I'll stop. Suffice it to say that Flutter is amazing! It is easy to write, elegant, and well designed – an absolute pleasure to code in.[2]

Conclusion

Now, if you're the kind of developer I hope you are, you're ready to get your hands dirty writing some code! So let's get to it. We'll start by installing and learning the Flutter development toolchain.

---

[2] But if you do want to read more, here's a deeper discussion of Flutter vs. some other frameworks: http://bit.ly/2HC9Khm

CHAPTER 2

Developing in Flutter

As we saw in the last chapter, Flutter enables us to create apps that run on the Web, on desktop computers, and on mobile devices (which really is the main draw). But wait a second, how exactly do we create these apps? What editor should we use? What is needed in the Flutter project? How do you compile the Dart source code? Do we need any other tools to support the project? How do you get it into a browser or on a device in order to test it out? Good questions, right?

Let's answer those questions and more in this chapter. Let's cover two significant topics:

1. Tools Needed – How to install and maintain the Flutter toolchain

2. The Development Process – How to create the app, run it, and debug it

---

Caution   By its nature, cross-platform app development tooling involves an awful lot of moving parts from various organizations, few of whom consult with the others before making changes. And since we're dealing with boundary-pushing and young technology, changes happen frequently. We've tried in this chapter to stick with timeless information but even it is likely to become stale eventually. Please check with the authors of these tools for the latest and greatest information.

© Rap Payne 2024
R. Payne, *Flutter App Development*, https://doi.org/10.1007/979-8-8688-0485-4_2

The Flutter Toolchain

There is no end to the list of helpful tools that the development community has produced. It is truly overwhelming. We're making no attempt at covering them all. We want to give you just enough for you to be proficient but not so many that you're overburdened. Forgive me if I've skipped your favorite.

The Flutter SDK

The Flutter SDK is the only indispensable tool. It includes the Flutter compiler, project creator, device manager, test runner, and tools that diagnose – and even correct – problems with the Flutter configuration.

Installing the Flutter SDK

The installation instructions are found here: `https://flutter.dev/docs/get-started/install`. Long story short – it will involve downloading the latest zip file of tools and setting your PATH to point to the folder where you unzipped them. The steps vary per operating system, but they're very plain on that website.

Tip This step seems very low level and sounds intimidating, but after this step, things get easier and less error prone. Don't let it discourage you.

IDEs

In theory, an IDE isn't really needed. Flutter can be written using any editor and then compiled and run using the Flutter SDK that you installed earlier. But in reality, almost nobody ever does that. Why would they? The following IDEs have Flutter support built right in!

VS Code from Microsoft

VS Code is from Microsoft. Its official name is "Microsoft Visual Studio Code," but most of us just call it *VS Code*. Whatever you call it, please do not confuse it with Microsoft's other product called "Microsoft Visual Studio." They are not the same thing regardless of the similar names.

You can get VS Code here: `https://code.visualstudio.com`.

Android Studio/IntelliJ from JetBrains

Android Studio and IntelliJ are essentially the same thing. They are built from the same codebase and have the same features.

You can get Android Studio at `https://developer.android.com/studio` and IntelliJ IDEA here: `www.jetbrains.com/idea/download`.

Which IDE Should I Use?

Both VS Code and Android Studio/IntelliJ are free and open source. Both run cross-platform on Windows, Mac, and Linux. Both are roughly equally popular with Flutter developers,[1] neither having a clear market advantage over the other. You can't go wrong with either one.

But if you must choose one, what we've found is that your background may affect how you like the tools. Developers from the web development world, those who use tech like HTML, CSS, JavaScript, NodeJS, React, Angular, or Vue, strongly prefer VS Code. On the other hand, those developers who came from a Java world, especially Android developers, seem to lean toward Android Studio/IntelliJ.

---

[1] A poll of Flutter devs by Andrew Brogdon (@redbrogdon) of the Flutter team showed that 53% use VS Code, 30% use Android Studio, and 15% use IntelliJ. See `http://bit.ly/flutter_devtools_poll`

The good news is that this is a very low-pressure choice. It is trivial to switch editors – even while working on a given project. Start in one and see how you like it. If you don't, you can give the other a test drive for a while. Go back and forth a couple of times until you have a strong preference. It's really no big deal to switch.

IDE DevTools

While those IDEs are great, they're not built for Flutter exclusively; they're used for developing in other languages and frameworks as well. So to improve the Flutter development flow, we should install the Flutter DevTools. It adds in debugger support, lets you look at logs, connects seamlessly with emulators, and a few more things.

Installing the DevTools is done from *within* each IDE. Within Android Studio/IntelliJ, go to "Preferences ➤ Plugins" from the main menu (Figure 2-1). In VS Code, go to "View ➤ Extensions" (Figure 2-2). The Flutter DevTools are simply called "Flutter," and a search will turn them up. In either platform, hit the green "Install" button.

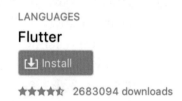

Figure 2-1. *DevTools install in Android Studio*

Figure 2-2. *DevTools install in VS Code*

You may need to restart the IDE after you install.

Emulators

Once you've got the IDE and DevTools installed, you're ready to compile your app. To run it, let's get it on a device. An emulator – a virtual device that runs on your laptop/desktop – makes it really easy to run, test, debug, and show your app. You'll probably want to test on both iOS and Android, so you'll want emulators for each. There are several emulators available, but I'll mention just a couple, Xcode's iOS simulator and AVD's Android emulator.

iOS Simulator

If you don't own a Mac, you won't be running an iOS emulator or even compiling for iOS for that matter.[2] But if you do and you have Xcode installed, you're in luck; you have the iOS simulator already. To run it, you open Xcode, then go to Xcode ➤ Open Developer Tool ➤ Simulator (Figure 2-3). The simulator will start up, and from within it, you can select any iOS device including iPhones and iPads.

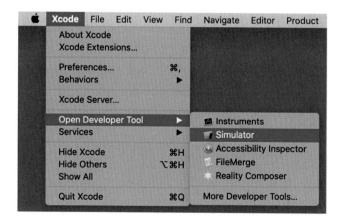

Figure 2-3. *Opening the iOS simulator from Xcode*

---

[2] <sarcasm>Thanks, Apple.</sarcasm>

Android Emulator

Just like there are tons of Android models, so are there tons of Android emulators, but there is only one popular ways to interact with them: AVD (Android Virtual Device) Manager. The AVD Manager is found in Android Studio under Tools (Figure 2-4).

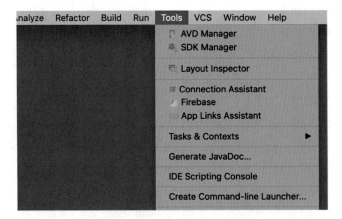

Figure 2-4. *Finding the AVD Manager in Android Studio*

Once opened, you'll see a list of your currently installed emulators. It should start out empty at first. You'll have the ability to install one or more of the hundreds of Android device emulators available by hitting the "Create Device" button at the top (Figure 2-5).

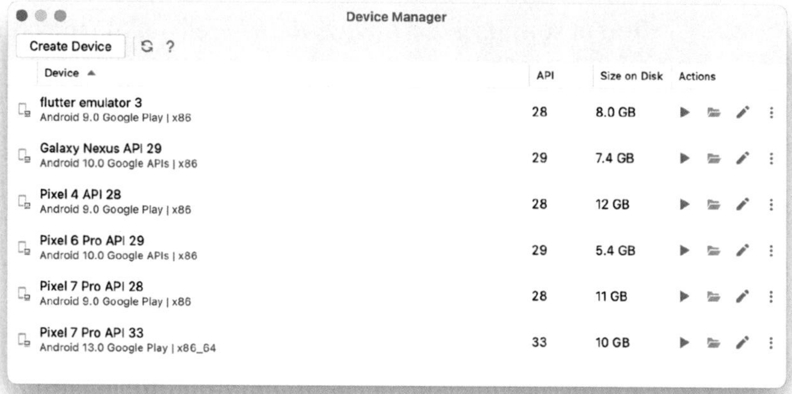

Figure 2-5. *AVD Manager has a list of available devices. Click "Create Device" to add more*

Hit it and you can choose from all kinds of devices or create one of your own. You'll only need to install a device once. After it's installed, that emulated device is usable from any IDE, whether IntelliJ/Android Studio or VS Code. No need for a separate setup on VS Code.

Keeping the Tools Up to Date

Early on, cross-platform development with tools like Xamarin and React Native was terribly difficult because of the sheer number of the tools involved and the interdependencies between them. I'm still in therapy from the pain.

But because Flutter arrived on the scene later, it can learn from others' mistakes. The Flutter team, recognizing these pain points, gave us an innovative tool to manage the rest of the toolchain. It will examine your development machine, looking for all the tools you'll need to develop Flutter apps, the versions you have, the versions that are available, and the interdependencies between them, and then make a diagnosis of problems.

It will even prescribe a solution to those problems. "Examine, diagnose, and prescribe?" Kind of sounds like a doctor, right? Well, let me introduce you to flutter doctor!

Flutter doctor

You'll run flutter doctor from the command line. It checks all the tools in your toolchain and reports back any problems it encounters. Here's one where Xcode needed some help:

```
$ flutter doctor
Doctor summary (to see all details, run flutter doctor -v):
[√] Flutter (Channel beta, vX.Y.Z, on Mac OS X X.Y.Z,
    locale en-US)
[√] Android toolchain - develop for Android devices (SDK
    version X.Y.Z)
[!] Xcode - develop for iOS and macOS (Xcode X.Y)
    X Xcode requires additional components to be installed in
      order to run.
      Launch Xcode and install additional required components
      when prompted.
[√] Android Studio (version X.Y)
[√] VS Code (version X.Y.Z)
[!] Connected device
    ! No devices available
! Doctor found issues in 2 categories.
$
```

The "No devices available" error is common, and you can usually ignore that one. It just means that at that moment no emulators were running.

Here's an example of what we prefer to see – everything checks out:

```
$ flutter doctor
Doctor summary (to see all details, run flutter doctor -v):
[√] Flutter (Channel beta, vX.Y.Z, on Mac OS X X.Y.Z,
    locale en-US)
[√] Android toolchain - develop for Android devices (SDK
    version X.Y.Z)
[√] Xcode - develop for iOS and macOS (Xcode X.Y)
[√] Android Studio (version X.Y)
[√] VS Code (version X.Y.Z)
[√] Connected device (1 available)
• No issues found!
```

flutter doctor not only detects and reports problems but it usually prescribes the fix for each. It will even tell you when it is time to upgrade itself via "flutter upgrade."

Flutter Upgrade

Yes, the initial installation of the Flutter SDK was a little daunting, but the upgrade is a breeze. You'll literally type two words, "flutter upgrade":

```
$ flutter upgrade
Upgrading Flutter from /usr/local/bin/flutter...
From https://github.com/flutter/flutter
   2d2a1ff..a72edc2  beta        -> origin/beta
   3932ffb..cc3ca9a  dev         -> origin/dev
   5a3a46a..a085635  master      -> origin/master
 * [new branch]      refactor    -> origin/refactor
<snip>
* [new tag]          vX.A.B      -> vX.Y.Z
Updating c382b8e..a72edc2
 11 files changed, 413 insertions(+), 302 deletions(-)
```

```
Building flutter tool...
Upgrading engine...
Downloading ios-deploy...                              0.3s
Flutter X.Y.Z • channel beta • https://github.com/flutter/
flutter.git
Framework • revision a72e06 (23 hours ago) • 20XX-YY-ZZ
15:41:01 -0700
Engine • revision b863200c37
Tools • Dart X.Y.Z
Running flutter doctor...
Doctor summary (to see all details, run flutter doctor -v):
[√] Flutter (Channel beta, vX.Y.Z, on Mac OS X X.Y.Z,
    locale en-US)
[√] Android toolchain - develop for Android devices (SDK
    version X.Y.Z)
[√] Xcode - develop for iOS and macOS (Xcode X.Y)
[√] Android Studio (version X.Y)
[√] VS Code (version X.Y.Z)
[√] Connected device (1 available)
• No issues found!
```

Note that flutter doctor is automatically run as the last step, confirming that all is well. Upgrading is a piece of cake.

The Flutter Development Process

Now that we have all the tools installed and up to date; let's create an app and run it through the debugger.

Scaffolding the App and Files

Create a whole new Flutter app by running ...

```
$ flutter create my_app
```

This will create a subfolder under the current folder called my_app. It will be full of ready-to-run Dart code.

Tip   The app name is case insensitive, so you should make it all lowercase. Dashes are illegal characters, so you can't use kebab-casing. The recommended casing is lowercase_with_underscores.

Anatomy of a Flutter Project

It's not critical that you know about all of the files and folders that are in the project you just created. But if you're curious, let's quickly walk through a newly created Flutter project shown in Figure 2-6.

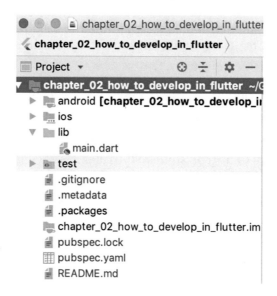

Figure 2-6. *A fresh Flutter project made by flutter create*

You'll have these folders:

- android, ios, web, linux, windows, macos – These are the platform-specific parts of the project. You won't need to touch these unless you're doing something to make your app run differently on different platforms.

- lib – This is the home of all of your Dart source code. You will build your app's hierarchy here. This is where you'll spend nearly all of your time and attention.

- test – If you have unit tests (and you probably should eventually), put them here.

And you'll have these files:

- pubspec.yaml – This is essentially the project file for Dart projects. This is where we set our project name, description, dependencies, and more. Be sure to read the comments in here to get a better picture of what is suggested and possible.

- .gitignore and README.md – These will be very familiar to devs who use Git and GitHub for their source code repository. Others won't care.

- analysis_options.yaml – Linting rules and setup for your project. This instructs the IDE how to warn you when you write ugly code. If it is too aggressive and you want to turn off some of the rules, just delete the lines or comment them out. An explanation of all of the linting rules can be found here: `http://dart-lang.github.io/linter/lints/`.

Running Your App

You now have a Flutter app created. Let's go run it. There are multiple ways of running your app. The most popular way is to hit the green "Play" button in either Android Studio/IntelliJ or VS Code (Figure 2-7). You'll have the option of debugging your app by setting breakpoints and stepping through the code using the developer tools (Figure 2-8).

Figure 2-7. *The Play and Debug buttons are at the top in Android Studio*

Figure 2-8. *The Play button is in the upper left in VS Code*

Obviously, you'll need to run your app in a device of some kind. There are several: the Chrome browser for a web app, emulators, or a physical device that is tethered to your development machine via a cable. When you click the Play/Debug button, you get to choose which device you want to run at that moment. Notice that in the preceding screenshot of Android Studio, there's a dropdown menu with a list of available devices. In VS Code, hit the Play button, and a menu immediately pops up with your choices. With either IDE, you are in control.

Tip   You can check what devices are currently available to you by running "flutter devices" from the command line.

```
$ flutter devices
3 connected devices:
Vivo XL3    • 55S...KF • android-arm64 • Android 8.0.0 (API 26)
Android SDK • emul...4 • android-x86   • Android 9 (API 28)
iPhone X    • E6...39A • ios • com.apple...OS-12-1 (simulator)
```

The preceding sample output tells us that we have three devices. The first and second are Android devices and the third runs iOS. The first device is a tethered physical device. The second and third are emulators.

Note that this command is different from the "flutter emulators" command which tells you all *possible* emulators you could potentially choose from. The flutter devices command tells you which devices are *currently* available to run your app.

Running It As a Web App

This is the easiest option. Flutter considers your browser to be a device when you're running as a web app. So all that is needed to run as a web app is to enable the Google Chrome web browser as a device. When you get a list of devices on which to run your app, "Chrome" will appear as one of them. Simply choose to run your app in Chrome and the IDE will load your web app in it.

Running It on a Tethered Device

There are times when you need to run your app on a physical device. For example, I was developing a project that involved printing labels to a physical printer connected by Bluetooth. Emulators don't pair via Bluetooth. To test the printing, I needed an actual physical device that was already paired to my Bluetooth printer.

To tether a physical device to your development machine, you'll use a physical cable.

Tips   #1 When connecting an Android device, it will initially think you're trying to charge it or transfer photos. To let it know you're trying to debug, open the Developer Options screen on the device and select "Enable USB debugging."

#2 Many connection issues can be caused by an inferior cable. Counterintuitively, not all cables are created equal. Switch to a higher-quality cable if you still can't connect after changing settings.

Hot Reloading

The initial compile may be a little slow. But once the app is running in your emulator/browser/physical device/whatever, you'll make changes to the source code and rerun. Here's the really cool thing: any time you save a change to the source code, it is recompiled and the new version is loaded instantly. Your app picks up where you left off – in the same spot, with the same state, and same data. We call it "hot reloading," and it makes the development cycle ridiculously fast and frictionless.

Debugging

Both IDEs have essentially the same debugging tools you've become accustomed to in all IDEs. When you start your project running, the debugging tools will appear.

In Android Studio, the debug window opens, usually at the bottom of the IDE. It has a tiny toolbar which looks like Figure 2-9.

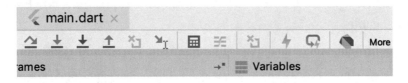

Figure 2-9. *The debugging toolbar in Android Studio*

The options are "step over," "step into," "force step into," and "step out" from left to right.

In VS Code, the toolbar appears floating over your source code (Figure 2-10).

Figure 2-10. *The debugging toolbar in VS Code*

Its options are "play/pause," "step over," "step into," "step out," "hot reload," "restart," and "stop debugging."

Note   Flutter is pickier when you're debugging than when running for real in a device. This is a good thing because during debugging, it makes obvious certain errors that you should probably fix but aren't necessarily fatal. In the release version, it swallows those same errors and (hopefully) allows our users to continue running our app.

One family of those errors is "runtime assertions." You'll know you're dealing with one of these when the debugger gives you an error like this:

```
================= Exception caught by gesture =================
The following assertion was thrown while handling a gesture:
setState() callback argument returned a Future.
The setState() method on _FooState#236 was called with a
closure or method that returned a Future. Maybe it is marked as
"async".
etc. etc. etc.
```

Your takeaway is this: when you see one of these, fix the problem. It's the right thing to do. But don't be confused if you don't see that same problem after you've deployed it.

Conclusion

Look, I know that this is a lot of stuff to absorb. The nature of cross-platform development makes the tooling hairy. But the worst is behind us. Once you've got the Flutter SDK and an IDE (VS Code/Android Studio/IntelliJ IDEA) installed, that's all you really need. And granted, the DevTools and an emulator or two can really help. All that's left is getting some repetitions in for practice. You're going to be great!

So now that we've seen the Flutter toolchain, let's start creating widgets!

CHAPTER 3

Everything Is Widgets

Let's pretend that you are an insanely talented Lego nerd and got offered one of the few coveted jobs as a Lego Master Builder. Congrats! Let's also say that your first assignment is to build a six-foot-tall Thor made from 26,000 Legos (Figure 3-1).

Figure 3-1. *A Lego Thor. The author snapped this picture at a movie theater once*

R. Payne, *Flutter App Development*, https://doi.org/10.1007/979-8-8688-0485-4_3

How would you go about doing that? Ponder that for a minute. Go ahead, we'll wait.

Would you just start grabbing bricks and putting them together? Probably not. Would you lay out the soles of Thor's feet and build from the bottom up? Again, no. Here's my guess as to your commonsense strategy:

1. You'd get a vision of what you're building. Figure the whole thing out.

2. Realize that the entire project is too complex to build at once.

3. Break the project into sections (legs, left arm, right arm, torso, left sword, right sword, helmet, cape, head).

4. Realize that each of them is still too complex.

5. For each section, you break it into subsections.

6. Repeat steps 4 and 5 until you've got simple enough components that each is easy to understand, build, and maintain – for you and for any teammates that you may have.

7. Create each simple component.

8. Combine simple components to form the larger, more complex components.

9. Repeat steps 7 and 8 until you've got your entire project created.

This process has a name, *componentization*, and is exactly the thought process we'll go through with our Flutter apps.

Componentization is not something new. In fact, it was proposed as far back as 1968.[1] But the technique has recently exploded in popularity thanks to web frameworks like Angular, React, Vue, Svelte, SolidJS, and native web components. Seems like all the cool kids are doing software components these days. The idea of recursively breaking down the complex bits into simpler bits is called *decomposition*. And the act of putting the written pieces back together into larger components is called *composition*.

In the world of Flutter, these components are referred to as *widgets*. Flutter people like to say "everything is widgets," meaning that you and I will be using the built-in widgets that ship with Flutter. We'll compose them together to create our own custom widgets. And our custom widgets will be composed together to create more and more complex custom widgets. This continues until you've got yourself a full-blown app.

Every app can be thought of in two parts:

1.   Behavior – What the software does. All of the business logic goes here: the data reading, writing, and processing.

2.   Presentation – How the software looks. The user interface. The buttons, textboxes, and labels.

Only Flutter combines these into one language instead of two.

---

[1] http://bit.ly/componentHistory

UI As Code

Other development frameworks have proven componentization to be the way to go. The Flutter team has openly stated that they were heavily inspired by React[2] which is based on componentization. In fact, all framework makers seem to borrow heavily from one another. But Flutter is unique in the way that the user interface is expressed. Developers use the same Dart language to express an app's graphical user interface as well as the behavior (Table 3-1). We call this "UI as code."

Table 3-1. *Only Flutter uses the same language for presentation and behavior*

Framework	Behavior expressed in …	UI expressed in …
Maui	C#	XAML
React Native	JavaScript	JSX
NativeScript	JavaScript	XML
Flutter	Dart	Dart

So how does this UI get created? Like many other frameworks and languages, a flutter app starts with a *main* function. In Flutter, main will call a function called runApp(). This runApp() receives one widget, the root widget which can be named anything, but it should be a class that extends a Flutter Stateful/StatelessWidget. It looks like this:

```
// import the Dart package needed for all Flutter apps
import 'package:flutter/material.dart';

// Here is main calling runApp
void main() => runApp(RootWidget());
```

---

[2] Source: https://flutter.dev/docs/resources/faq#does-flutter-come-with-a-framework

28

```
// And here is your root widget
class RootWidget extends StatelessWidget {
  @override
  Widget build(BuildContext context) {
    return Text("Hello world");
  }
}
```

And that's all you need to create a "Hello world" in Flutter.

But wait ... what is this Text() thing? It's a built-in Flutter widget. Since these built-in widgets are so important, we need to take a look at them.

Built-In Flutter Widgets

Flutter's foundational widgets are the building blocks of everything we create, and there are tons of them – over 1300 at last count.[3] This is a lot of widgets for you and I to know. But if you mentally organize them, it becomes much more manageable.

They fall into these major categories:

- Value widgets

- Layout widgets

- Navigation widgets

- Other widgets

---

[3] You can find a list of them all here: https://flutter.dev/docs/reference/widgets

29

Note   These are not Flutter's official list of categories. Their 15 categories are listed here: `https://flutter.dev/docs/development/ui/widgets`. We just felt that reorganizing them helps to keep them straight.

We'll take a brief look at each of these categories with an example or two, and then we'll do some deep dives in later chapters. Let's start with value widgets.

Value Widgets

Certain widgets hold a value, maybe values that came from local storage, a service on the Internet, or from the user themselves. These are used to display values to the user and to get values from the user into the app. The seminal example is the Text widget which displays a little bit of text. Another is the Image widget which displays a .jpg, .png, or another picture.

Here are some more value widgets:

AlertDialog	FloatingActionButton	RawImage RefreshIndicator
Badge	FlutterLogo	RichText
Checkbox	Form	SegmentedButton
Chip	FormField	Slider
CircularProgressIndicator	Icon	SnackBar
Date & Time Pickers	IconButton	Switch
DataTable	Image	Text
DropdownButton	LinearProgressIndicator	TextField
ElevatedButton	Menu	Tooltip
FlatButton	PopupMenuButton	
	Radio	

We'll explore value widgets in more detail in the next chapter.

Layout Widgets

Layout widgets give us tons of control in making our scene lay out properly – placing widgets side by side with a Row widget or above and beneath, with a Column widget making them scrollable with a SingleChildScrollView, making them wrap with Wrap, determining the space around widgets with Padding so they don't feel crowded, and so on:

Align	Flow	Placeholder
AppBar	FractionallySizedBox	Row
AspectRatio	GridView	Scaffold
BottomAppBar	IntrinsicHeight	Scrollable
BottomSheet	IntrinsicWidth	Scrollbar
Card	LayoutBuilder	SingleChildScrollView
Center	LimitedBox	SizedBox
Column	ListTile	SizedOverflowBox
ConstrainedBox	ListView	Slivers*
Container	MediaQuery	SnackBar
Divider	NestedScrollview	Stack
Expanded	OverflowBox	Table
ExpansionPanel	Padding	Transform
FittedBox	PageView	Wrap

This is a huge topic which we're covering in the final six chapters of the book.

Navigation Widgets

When your app has multiple scenes ("screens," "pages," whatever you want to call them), you'll need some way to move between them. That's where navigation widgets come in. These will control how your user sees one scene and then moves to the next. Usually this is done when the user taps a button. And sometimes the navigation button is located on a tab bar or in a drawer that slides in from the left side of the screen. Here are some navigation widgets:

AlertDialog	NavigationDrawer	SimpleDialog
Drawer	NavigationRail	TabBar
MaterialApp	Navigator	TabBarView
NavigationBar		

We'll learn how they work in Chapter 6, "Navigation and Routing."

Other Widgets

And no, not all widgets fall into these neat categories. Let's lump the rest into a miscellaneous category. Here are some miscellaneous widgets:

ClipPath	FutureBuilder GestureDetector	StreamBuilder
Cupertinos*	Semantics*	Theme
Dismissible		Transitions*

Many of these miscellaneous widgets are covered throughout the book where they fit naturally. GestureDetector and Dismissible appear in Chapter 5, "Responding to Gestures." Theme is covered in Chapter 10, "Styling with Themes." FutureBuilder and StreamBuilder are in Chapter 9, "Making RESTful API Calls with HTTP."

How to Create Your Own Stateless Widgets

So we know that we will be composing these built-in widgets to form our own custom widgets which will then be composed with other built-in widgets to eventually form an app.

Widgets are masterfully designed because each widget is easy to understand and therefore easy to maintain. Widgets are abstract from the outside while being logical and predictable on the inside. They are a dream to work with.

Every widget is a class that can have properties and methods. Every widget can have a constructor with zero or more parameters. And most importantly, every widget has a *build* method which receives a BuildContext[4] and returns a single Flutter widget.

Tip   If you're ever wondering how a widget got to look the way it does, locate its build method.

```
class RootWidget extends StatelessWidget {
  @override
  Widget build(BuildContext context) {
    return Text('Hello world');
  }
}
```

In this hello world example which we repeated from earlier in the chapter, we're displaying a Text widget (Figure 3-2). A single inner widget works but real-world apps will be a whole lot more complex. The root widget could be composed of many other subwidgets:

```
class FancyHelloWidget extends StatelessWidget {
  Widget build(BuildContext context) {
    return MaterialApp(
      home: Scaffold(
```

---

[4] Don't get distracted by the BuildContext. It's used by the framework and we do occasionally refer to it, but we'll save those examples later in the book. For now, just think of it as part of the recipe to write a custom widget.

```
    appBar: AppBar(
      title: Text("A fancier app"),
    ),
    body: Container(
      alignment: Alignment.center,
      child: Text("Hello world"),
    ),
    floatingActionButton: FloatingActionButton(
      child: Icon(Icons.thumb_up),
      onPressed: () => {},
    ),
  ),
);
  }
}
```

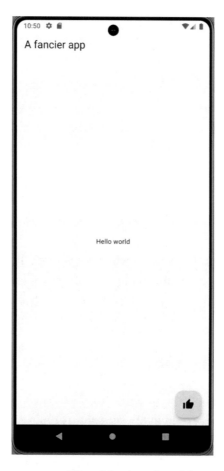

Figure 3-2.   *The app created by this simple widget*

So as you can see, the build method is returning a single widget, a MaterialApp, but it contains a Scaffold which contains three subwidgets: an AppBar, a Container, and a FloatingActionButton (Figure 3-3). Each of those in turn contains sub-subwidgets of their own.

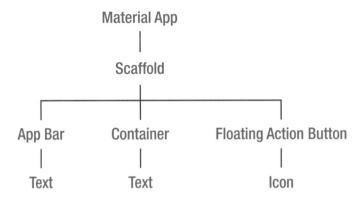

Figure 3-3. *The widget tree from our example app above*

This is how your build method will always work. It will return a single, massive, nested expression. It is widgets inside widgets inside widgets that enable you to create your own elaborate custom widget.

Widgets Have Keys

Let's talk Flutter architecture for a minute. Flutter would be slow if it tried to re-render the entire screen every time a tiny change was made. Instead, Flutter applies state changes to an in-memory copy of the screen called the element tree. This is very fast because they're not actually painted on the screen. The painting is reserved for the "render tree."

Well, here's the beauty of this structure – when the render tree is drawn, it reuses all the widgets that have *not* changed since the last render. Only those widgets that need a re-render get a re-render. But how does Flutter know? It uses keys.

Every widget has a unique key. It gets one automatically but you may assign the key manually if you prefer. When a widget needs to redraw, it is recreated in memory and gets a new key. Flutter assumes that any widget whose type and key have not changed can be left alone.

But occasionally, Flutter gets confused when matching the widgets in the element trees. You'll know to manually assign keys if your widgets get drawn in the wrong location, the data isn't updated on the screen, or your scroll position isn't preserved.

Typically you don't need to worry about keys. They're needed so rarely that we're going to be satisfied if you understand that ...

1. Keys exist and why Flutter may need them.

2. Keys may solve problems when your widgets aren't being redrawn as you might expect.

3. You have the opportunity to assign keys to widgets.

If that's not enough to satisfy you for now, the great Emily Fortuna has recorded a super 10-minute video on keys.[5]

Passing a Value into Your Widget

Do you know what this formula means?

$$y = f(x)$$

Math majors will recognize this as reading "*y* is a function of *x*." It concisely communicates that as *x* (the independent variable) changes, *y* (the dependent variable) will change in a predictable way. Flutter lives on this idea, but in Flutter, the formula reads like this:

$$Scene = f(Data)$$

In other words, as the data in your app changes, the screen will change accordingly. And you, the developer, get to decide how that data is presented as you write a build method in your widgets. It is a foundational concept of Flutter.

---

[5] You can find Emily's video here: `http://bit.ly/FlutterKeys`

Now how might that data change? There are two ways:

1.   The widget can be re-rendered with new data passed from outside.

2.   Data can be maintained *within* certain widgets.

Let's talk about the first. To pass data into a widget, you'll send it in as constructor parameters:

```
Widget build(BuildContext context) {
  return Person(firstName: "Sarah", lastName: "Ali");
}
```

Here's how you'd write your widget to receive that value:

```
class Person extends StatelessWidget {
  final String firstName;
  final String lastName;
  Person({this.firstName = "", this.lastName = ""}) {}
  @override
  Widget build(BuildContext context) {
    return Text('$firstName $lastName');
  }
}
```

We're passing the first and last name in to the widget. There are other ways of writing a Dart constructor. Take a look at Appendix A, "Dart Language Overview," or a Dart reference to see them.

Tip   Note that in the preceding example, we are using a Person class that might have been defined in the same dart file where you're using it. But a better practice is to create each class in a separate dart file and import it into other dart files where it is used.

```
import 'Person.dart';
```

State*less* and State*ful* Widgets

So far we've been going out of our way to create stateless widgets. So you probably guessed that there's also a stateful widget. You were right. A state*less* widget is one that doesn't maintain its own state. A state*ful* widget does.

"State" in this context refers to data within the widget that can change during its lifetime. Think about our Person widget from earlier. If it's a widget that just displays the person's information, it should be stateless. But if it is a person **maintenance** widget where we allow the user to change the data by typing into a TextField, then we'd need a StatefulWidget.

There's a whole chapter on stateful widgets later. If you just can't wait to know more about them, you can read Chapter 7, "Managing State," later in this book. Then come back here.

So Which One Should I Create?

The short answer is create a stateless widget. Never use a stateful widget until you must. Assume all widgets you make will be stateless and start them out that way. Refactor them into stateful widgets when you're sure you really do need state. But recognize that state can be avoided more often than developers think. Avoid it when you can to make widgets simpler and therefore easier to write, to maintain, and to extend. Your team members will thank you for it.

Note   There is actually a third type of widget, the InheritedWidget. You set a value in your InheritedWidget and any descendent can reach back up through the tree and ask for that data directly. You can read more about it in Chapter 8, "State Management Libraries," or watch a concise overview of InheritedWidget here: `http://bit.ly/inheritedWidget`.

Conclusion

So now we know that Flutter apps are all about widgets. You'll compose your own custom stateless or stateful widgets that have a build method which will render a tree of built-in Flutter widgets. So clearly we need to know about the built-in Flutter widgets which we'll learn beginning in the next chapter.

CHAPTER 4

Value Widgets

We learned in the last chapter that *everything is a widget.* Everything you create is a widget, and everything that Flutter provides us is a widget. Sure, there are exceptions to that, but it never hurts to think of it this way, especially as you're getting started in Flutter. In this chapter, we're going to drill down into the most fundamental group of widgets that Flutter provides us – the ones that hold a value. We'll talk about the Text widget, the Icon widget, and the Image widget, all of which display exactly what their names imply. We'll briefly glance at the SnackBar widget. Then we'll dive into the input widgets – ones designed to get input from the user.

The Text Widget

If you want to display a string to the screen, the Text widget is what you'll need. It takes a string as input, the actual text you want to show, and displays it on the screen. By default, it shows everything on a single line, but if the container isn't wide enough, it will naturally wrap to multiple lines.

```
Widget build(BuildContext context) {
  String str = 'Hello world';
  return Text(str);
}
```

R. Payne, *Flutter App Development*, https://doi.org/10.1007/979-8-8688-0485-4_4

Tip   If your Text is a literal, put the word const in front of it and the widget will be created at compile time instead of runtime. Your apk/ipa file will be slightly larger, but they'll run faster on the device. Well worth it.

You have control over the Text's size, font, weight, color, and more with its style property. But we'll cover that in Chapter 10, "Styling with Themes."

Text() handles most of your single-style text needs. But what if you want different parts of the text to have different styles? That's where RichText comes in. It allows you to mix and match styles within the same text widget using TextSpan objects.

The Icon Widget

Flutter comes with a huge set of built-in icons (Figure 4-1), from cameras to people to cards to vehicles to arrows to batteries to Android/iOS devices. A full list can be found here: `https://api.flutter.dev/flutter/material/Icons-class.html`, but that's not easy to search. So here's a place to search by name: `https://fonts.google.com/icons`.

Figure 4-1. *An assortment of Flutter's built-in widgets in random colors*

To place an icon, you use the Icon widget. No surprise there. You use the Icons class to specify which one. This class has hundreds of static values like Icons.phone_android and Icons.phone_iphone and Icons.cake. Each points to a different icon like the ones pictured previously. Here's how you'd put a big red birthday cake (Figure 4-2) on your app:

```
Icon(
  Icons.cake,
  color: Colors.red,
  size: 200,
)
```

Figure 4-2. *The red cake icon*

If the almost 9,000 built-in icons are not enough for you, it is very possible to use other icon sets. Font Awesome is available for Flutter at `https://pub.dev/packages/font_awesome_flutter`. It makes another 2,000 icons available. And the icons_flutter package at `https://pub.dev/packages/icons_flutter` has another 14,000. That should tide you over for a while.

The Image Widget

Displaying images in Flutter is a bit more complex than Text or Icons. It involves a few things:

1. Getting the Image Source – This could be an image embedded in the app itself or fetched live from the Internet. If the image will never change through the life of your app like a logo or decorations, it should be an embedded image.

2. Sizing It – Scaling it up or down to the right size and shape.

Embedded Images

Embedded images are much faster at run time but will increase your app's install size at compile time. To embed the image, put the image file in your project folder. Anywhere in your project will be fine but the convention is to put it in a subfolder called assets, probably in a sub-subfolder just to keep things straight. Something like assets/images will do nicely.

Then edit pubspec.yaml. Add this to it:

```
flutter:
  assets:
    - assets/images/photo1.png
    - assets/images/photo2.jpg
```

Save the file and run "flutter pub get" from the command line to have your project process the file.

Tip   The pubspec.yaml file holds all kinds of great information about your project. It holds project metadata like the name, description, repository location, and version number. It lists library dependencies and fonts. It is the go-to location for other developers new to your project. For any of you JavaScript developers, it is the package.json file of your Dart project. See Appendix C, "Including Packages in your Flutter App," for more information.

You'll put the image in your widget by calling the asset() constructor like this:

```
Image.asset('assets/images/photo1.jpg'),
```

Network Images

Network images are much more like what web developers might be accustomed to. It is simply fetching an image over the Internet via HTTP. You'll use the network constructor and pass in a URL as a string.

```
Image.network(imageUrl),
```

As you'd expect, these are slower than embedded images because there's a delay while the request is being sent to a server over the Internet and the image is being downloaded by your device. The advantage is that these images are live; any image can be loaded dynamically by simply changing the image URL.

Sizing an Image

Images are nearly always put in a container. Not that this is a requirement, it's just that I can't imagine a real-world use case where it won't be inside another widget. The container has a say in the size that an image is drawn. It would be an amazing coincidence if the image's natural size fit its container's size perfectly. Instead, Flutter's layout engine will shrink the image to fit its container, but not grow it. This fit is called *BoxFit. scaleDown*, and it makes sense for the default behavior. But what other options are available and how do we decide which to use? Table 4-1 provides your BoxFit options.

Table 4-1. *BoxFit options*

fill	Stretch it so that both the width and the height fit exactly. It may distort the image	
cover	Shrink or grow until the space is filled. The top/ bottom or sides may be clipped. Does not distort the image	
fitHeight	Make the height fit exactly. Clip the width or add extra space as needed	
fitWidth	Make the width fit exactly. Clip the height or add extra space as needed	
contain	Shrink until both the height *and* the width fit. There may be extra space on the top/bottom or sides	 

Photo courtesy of Eye for Ebony on Unsplash

So those are your options, but how do you choose? Figure 4-3 may help you decide which fit to use in different situations.

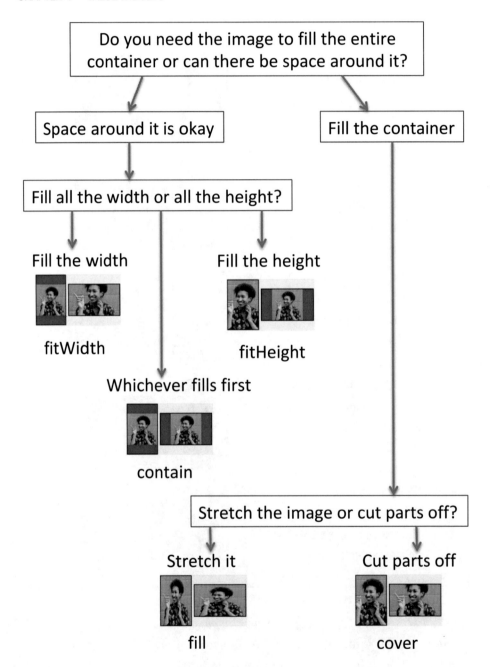

Figure 4-3. *How to decide an image's fit*

To specify the fit, you'll set the *fit* property.

```
Image.asset('assets/images/woman.jpg', fit: BoxFit.contain,),
```

SnackBar Widget

Weird name, I know. Sounds like something delicious, but this widget is really a standard way to alert your user to something. A SnackBar (Figure 4-4) will appear at the bottom of your screen, occulting whatever is already down there and will disappear after a short time. You get to decide what the SnackBar says, and you can even place a button on it for the user to take action.

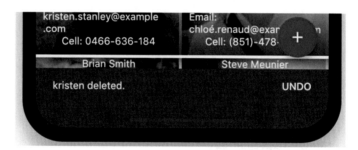

Figure 4-4. *A SnackBar shows a message and optional actions*

You can show a SnackBar in any scene you like as long as you do it in a widget that is nested inside a Scaffold. You must

1. Create the Snackbar

2. Call ScaffoldMessenger.of(context). showSnackBar(sb)

3. Handle the action button (optional)

Note that showSnackBar() runs asynchronously so as to not block the UI thread. It will stay up for four seconds by default but that can be overridden by the duration property. Here's an example:

```
IconButton(
  icon: const Icon(Icons.delete, size: 36),
  onPressed: () {
    bool goAheadAndDeletePerson = true;
    final SnackBar sb = SnackBar(
      content: Text("${person.name} deleted."),
      duration: const Duration(seconds: 5),
      action: SnackBarAction(
        label: "UNDO",
        onPressed: () => goAheadAndDeletePerson = false,
      ),
    );
    ScaffoldMessenger.of(context).showSnackBar(sb);
    Future.delayed(const Duration(seconds: 5), () {
      if (goAheadAndDeletePerson) {
        deletePerson(person);
      }
    });
  },
),
```

In this example, we're lying to the user ☺. We're telling them that the record has already been deleted but they really have five seconds to cancel that by hitting UNDO. The Future.delayed() says to run deletePerson() in a separate isolate after a five-second delay. If they hit UNDO within that timeframe, the Future skips the delete.

Of course you may just want to bring up a message only with no action. It's up to you.

Input Widgets

Many of us came from a web background where from the very beginning there were HTML <form>s with <input>s and <select>s. All of these exist to enable the user to get data into web apps, an activity we can't live without in mobile apps as well. Flutter provides widgets for entering data like we have on the Web, but they don't work the same way. They take much more work to create and use. Sorry about that. On the plus side, though, they are also safer and give us much more control.

Part of the complication is that these widgets don't maintain their own state; you have to do it manually.

Another part of the complication is that input widgets are unaware of each other. In other words, they don't play well together until you group them with a Form widget. We eventually need to focus on the Form widget. But before we do, let's study how to create text fields, checkboxes, radio buttons, sliders, and dropdowns.

Caution   Input widgets are really tough to work with unless they are used within a StatefulWidget because by nature, they change state. Remember that we mentioned StatefulWidgets briefly in the last chapter and we're going to talk about them in depth in Chapter 7, "Managing State." But until then, please just take our word for it and put them in a stateful widget for now.

Text Fields

If all you have is a single textbox, you probably want a TextField widget.
Here's a simple example of the TextField widget with a Text label above it:

```
const Text('Search terms'),
TextField(
  initialValue: "Some initial value",
  onChanged: (val) => _searchTerm = val,
),
```

That onChanged property is an event handler that fires after every
keystroke. It receives a single value – a String. This is the value that the user
is typing. In this example, we're setting a local variable called _searchTerm
to whatever the user types.

Did you notice the Text('Search terms')? That is our lame attempt at
putting a label above the TextField. There's a much, much better way.
Check this out ...

Making Your TextField Fancy

There's a ton of options to make your TextField more useful – not infinite
options, but lots. And they're all available through the InputDecoration
widget (Figure 4-5):

```
return TextField(
  decoration: InputDecoration(
    labelText: 'Email',
    hintText: 'you@email.com',
    icon: Icon(Icons.contact_mail),
  ),
),
```

Figure 4-5. *A TextField with an InputDecoration*

Table 4-2 presents some more InputDecoration options.

Table 4-2. *InputDecoration options*

Property	Description
labelText	Appears above the TextField. Tells the user what this TextField is for
hintText	Light ghost text inside the TextField. Disappears as the user begins typing
errorText	Error message that appears below the TextField. Usually in red. It is set automatically by validation (covered later), but you can set it manually if you need to
icon	Draws an icon to the left of the entire TextField
prefixIcon	Draws one inside the TextField to the left
suffixIcon	Same as prefixIcon but to the far right

Password Boxes

To make it a password box (Figure 4-6), set obscureText property to true. As the user types, each character appears for a second and is replaced by a dot.

```
return TextField(
  obscureText: true,
  decoration: InputDecoration(
    labelText: 'Password',
  ),);
```

Figure 4-6. *A password box with obscureText*

Adjusting the Soft Keyboard

Want a special soft keyboard? No problem. Just use the keyboardType property. Results are shown in Figures 4-7 through 4-10.

```
return TextField(
  keyboardType: TextInputType.number,
);
```

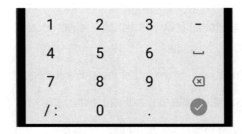

Figure 4-7. *TextInputType.datetime*

Figure 4-8. *TextInputType.email. Note the @ sign*

Figure 4-9. *TextInputType.number*

Figure 4-10. *TextInputType.phone*

The soft keyboard shows a different keyboard, but it doesn't control what can be put into each field. In other words, you can still get regular text into a FormField() even if the soft keyboard is of type number. Want to fix that? Here's how ...

Restricting the Data That Can Be Typed

If you want to limit the type of text that is allowed to be entered, you can do so with the TextInput's inputFormatters property. It's actually an array so you can combine one or more of ...

- BlacklistingTextInputFormatter – Forbids certain characters from being entered. They just don't appear when the user types.

- WhitelistingTextInputFormatter – Allows only these characters to be entered. Anything outside this list doesn't appear.

- LengthLimitingTextInputFormatter – Can't type more than X characters.

Those first two will allow you to use regular expressions to specify patterns that you want (white list) or don't want (black list). Here's an example:

```
return TextField(
  inputFormatters: [
    WhitelistingTextInputFormatter(RegExp('[0-9 -]')),
    LengthLimitingTextInputFormatter(16)
  ],
  decoration: InputDecoration(
    labelText: 'Credit Card',
  ),
);
```

In the WhitelistingTextInputFormatter, we're only allowing numbers 0–9, a space, or a dash. Then the LengthLimitingTextInputFormatter is keeping to a max of 16 characters.

Checkboxes

Flutter checkboxes (Figure 4-11) have a Boolean value property and an onChanged method which fires after every change. Like all of the other input widgets, the onChanged method receives the value that the user set. Therefore, in the case of Checkboxes, that value is a bool.

```
Checkbox(
  value: true,
  onChanged: (val) => print(val),
),
```

Figure 4-11. *A Flutter Checkbox widget*

Tip   A Flutter Switch (Figure 4-12) serves the same purpose as a Checkbox – it is on or off. So the Switch widget has the same options and works in the same way. It just looks different.

Figure 4-12. *A Flutter Switch widget*

Radio Buttons

Of course the magic in a radio button is that if you select one, the others in the same group are deselected. So obviously we need to group them somehow. In Flutter, Radio widgets are grouped when you set the groupValue property to the same local variable. This variable holds the value of the *one* Radio that is currently turned on.

Each Radio also has its own value property, the value associated with *that* particular widget whether it is selected or not. In the onChanged method, you'll set the groupValue variable to the radio's value.

value	Each radio has its own distinct value
groupValue	The one value currently selected, depending on which radio was last clicked.

Here's how they'd work together:

```
SearchLocation? searchLocation;
//Other code goes here
Radio(
    groupValue: searchLocation,
    value: SearchLocation.anywhere,
    onChanged: (val) => setState(() => searchLocation = val)),
const Text('Search anywhere'),
Radio(
    groupValue: searchLocation,
    value: SearchLocation.text,
    onChanged: (val) => setState(() => searchLocation = val)),
const Text('Search page text'),
Radio(
    groupValue: searchLocation,
    value: SearchLocation.title,
    onChanged: (val) => setState(() => searchLocation = val)),
const Text('Search page title'),
```

Note that each Radio has its own value, SearchLocation.anywhere for the first, SearchLocation.text for the second, and SearchLocation.title for the third. But they all share groupType which is what groups them together. Also note that when one is selected, its onChanged fires and we set the searchLocation variable to the selected option.

This simplified code would create something like Figure 4-13.

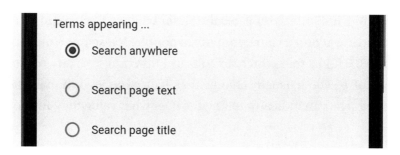

Figure 4-13. *Flutter Radio widgets*

Tip   Confused about SearchLocation? I don't blame you. It's an enumeration. Radios work really well with enums.

Here's how the above SearchLocation enum might be created:

enum SearchLocation { anywhere, title, text }

Sliders

A slider is a handy affordance when you want your user to pick a numeric value between an upper and lower limit (Figure 4-14).

Figure 4-14. *A slider with the value of 25*

To get one in Flutter, you'll use the Slider widget which requires an onChanged event and a value property, a double. It also has a min which defaults to 0.0 and a max which defaults to 1.0. A range of zero to one is rarely useful, so you'll usually change that. It also has an optional label property which is an indicator telling the user what value they're choosing.

```
Slider(
  label: numberOfResults.toString(),
  min: 0.0,
  max: 100.0,
  divisions: 100,
  value: numberOfResults.toDouble(),
  onChanged: (val) {
    setState(() => numberOfResults = val.round());
  },
);
```

Dropdowns

Dropdowns are great for picking one of a small number of things, like in an enumeration. Let's say we have an enum like this:

```
enum SearchType { web, image, news, shopping }
```

Where obviously we're defining a "SearchType" as either "web," "image," "news," or "shopping." If we wanted our user to choose from one of those, we might present them with a DropdownButton widget that might look like Figure 4-15 to start with.

Figure 4-15. DropdownButton with nothing chosen

Then, when they tap the dropdown, it looks like Figure 4-16.

Figure 4-16. *DropdownButton expanded to show the choices*

And when they tap one of the options, it is chosen (Figure 4-17).

Figure 4-17. *DropdownButton with an option selected*

To create that DropdownButton, our Flutter code might look like this:

```
SearchType searchType = SearchType.web;
//Other code goes here
return DropdownButton(
  value: searchType,
  items: [
    DropdownMenuItem(
      value: SearchType.web, child: Text('Web') ),
    DropdownMenuItem(
      value: SearchType.image, child: Text('Image') ),
```

```
    DropdownMenuItem(
      value: SearchType.news, child: Text('News') ),
    DropdownMenuItem(
      value: SearchType.shopping, child: Text('Shopping') ),
  ],
  onChanged: (val) => searchType = val,
);
```

Note that the items are all of type DropdownMenuItem. Those have a value and a child, but the onChanged event handler is on the Menu and not on the items. Kind of makes sense when you think about it.

Putting the Form Widgets Together

It's cool that we have all of these different types of fields that look good and work great. But you will often want them to be grouped together so that they can be somewhat controlled as a group. You'll do this with a Form widget.

Form Widget

In Flutter, a Form widget helps when you have multiple fields that depend on one another and/or if you have validations. That doesn't happen 100% of the time. So feel free to omit a Form widget if you don't need it. And feel free to skip reading this next section until you have a need to learn about the Form widget. Go to the next chapter. My feelings won't be hurt.

... Still here? Alright. Let's see what the Form widget can do for us. Strap in, because this ride gets bumpy ...

Forms need a GlobalKey. Remember that we introduced keys in the last chapter and told you that except in a few situations, keys can be ignored. This is one place where keys are needed. If you decide to use a Form, you need a GlobalKey of type FormState:

```
GlobalKey<FormState> _key = GlobalKey<FormState>();
```

You'll set that key as a property to your Form:

```
@override
Widget build(BuildContext context) {
  return Form(
    key: _key,
    autovalidate: AutovalidateMode.always,
    child: // All the form fields will go here
  );
}
```

At first glance, the Form doesn't seem to change anything. But a closer look reveals that we now have access to

- autovalidate – *always* means run validations as soon as any field changes. *disabled* means you'll run it manually. *onUserInteraction* means run them each time the user changes anything. (We'll talk about validations in a few pages.)

- The key itself which we called _key in the code above.

That _key has a *currentState* property which in turn has these methods:

1. save() – Saves all *fields* inside the form by calling each's onSaved

2. validate() – Runs each *field's* validator function

3. reset() – Resets each *field* inside the form back to its initialValue

63

Caution   currentState is a nullable property. This means we must use either "?" or "!" to placate the compiler. Remember, "?" means that if it's null, stop processing here (i.e., do nothing). And "!" means that we know it can never be null at this point. You'll see me using "!" for simplicity.

Armed with all this, you can see how the Form handles its nested fields. When you call one of these three methods, it iterates all inner fields and calls that method on each. One call at the Form level fires them all.

But hang on a second! If _key.currentState.save() is calling a field's onSaved(), we need to provide an onSaved method, right? Same with validate() calling the validator. But the TextField, DropdownButton, Radio, Checkbox, and Slider widgets themselves don't have those methods. What do we do now? We wrap each field in a *FormField* widget which **does** have those methods. (And the rabbit hole gets deeper.)

FormField Widget

This widget's entire purpose in life is to provide onSaved and validator event handlers to an inner widget. The FormField widget can wrap any widget using a builder property:

```
FormField<String>(
 builder: (state) {
  return TextField(); // Any field widget like Switch,
                      // Radio, Checkbox, or Slider.
 },
 onSaved: (String initialValue) {
  // Push values to a repository or something here.
 },
```

```
validator: (String val) {
  // Put validation logic here (further explained below).
},
),
```

So we first wrap a FormField widget around each input widget, and we do so in a method called *builder*. Then we can add the onSaved and validator methods.

Note   While Switches, Checkboxes, and Sliders are wrapped in a FormField, Radios are different. You're going to wrap the entire Radio group in a single FormField. This makes sense when you think about it – the group is determining one value – the groupValue.

TextFormField and DropdownButtonFormField

The Flutter team has kindly given us a shortcut. Instead of *wrapping* a TextField, *replace* it with a TextFormField widget if you use it inside a Form. This new widget is easy to confuse with a TextField but it is different. Basically …

TextFormField = TextField + FormField

TextFormField has all of the properties of a TextField but adds an onSaved and a validator:

```
TextFormField(
  initialValue: "Some initial string",
  decoration: InputDecoration(labelText: 'Email'),
  onSaved: (val) => print("Form saved: $val"),
  validator: (val) {
    // Put your validation logic here
  },
),
```

Similarly when using a DropdownButton in a Form, instead replace it with a DropdownButtonFormField:

```
DropdownButtonFormField<SearchType>(
 onChanged: (val) => _searchType = val,
 onSaved: (val) => _dbRecord["searchType"] == val,
 validator: _searchTypeValidator,
 value: _searchType,
 items: [...],
),
```

Now isn't that nicer? Finally, we catch a break in making things easier. Checkboxes don't have this shortcut. Nor do Radios nor Sliders. Only TextFields and DropDownButtons.

onSaved

Remember, your Form has a key which has a currentState which has a save() method. Got all that? No? Not super clear? Let's try it this way; on a "Save" button press, you will write code to call …

```
_key.currentState!.save();
```

… and it in turn invokes the onSaved method for each FormField in the Form.

validator

Similarly, you probably guessed that you can call …

```
_key.currentState!.validate();
```

... and Flutter will call each FormField's validator method. Each validator function will receive its value to be validated and return a nullable string. You'll write the function to return null if the input value is valid and an error message if it is invalid. That returned string is what Flutter will show your user:

```
return Form(
 child: TextFormField(
  validator: (val)=> (val == null || val.isEmpty)
        ? "Please enter some text"
        : null,
 ),
);
```

Submitting the Form

We're (finally) ready to actually submit the form. You'll usually do this on a button press, and you'll only want to submit the form if all the data is valid. Here's how that might look:

```
ElevatedButton(
  onPressed: () {
    if (_key.currentState!.validate()) {
      _key.currentState!.save();
      print("Form was saved.");
    }
  },
  child: const Text("Submit"),
);
```

One Big Form Example

I know, I know. This is pretty complex stuff. It might help to see these things in context – how they all fit together. Please look in the code repository for a file called search_form.dart which has all of these pieces combined in one big StatefulWidget.

Conclusion

It takes a while to understand Flutter forms. Please don't be discouraged. It begins to make sense very quickly as you work with forms. And while the topic of Forms might have been a little intimidating to you, Text, Images, Icons, and SnackBars were very straightforward, right?

In the next chapter, we'll start to see our app come alive because we're going to learn about creating all the different kinds of buttons and making them – or any widget for that matter – respond to taps and other gestures!

CHAPTER 5

Responding to Gestures

We've made great progress so far! You now know what Flutter is all about. You're well versed in how the development and debugging process works. You know why we use widgets and are pretty darn familiar with the value widgets from the last chapter. Heck, you can even create your own stateless widgets. But we're still missing a major fundamental feature: event handling.

Let's say you have a screen where the user chooses a product and puts it in their cart. They'll have to scroll up and down through a list of products (Figure 5-1). The swipe up and down to scroll is a gesture. To choose a product, they'll tap on it. That's a gesture. Then to put it in the cart, maybe we'd have them swipe right. That's a different gesture.

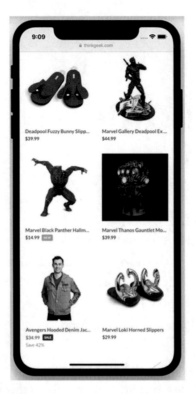

Figure 5-1. *A shopping app*

This chapter is all about handling those gestures. We'll fit gestures into two categories: gestures on built-in widgets and gestures on your custom widgets. Let's start with gesture on built-in widgets.

Meet the Button Family

Some gestures are super easy because they're pre-baked into certain widgets. For instance, the creators of button widgets know their sole purpose in life is to be pressed and then to do something in response to it. So all buttons come with a property called onPressed. To use it, you'll simply point it to a function to run when the user presses it:

```
IconButton(
  icon: const Icon(Icons.delete),
  // The callback function must return void
  onPressed: () => print("tapped"),
)
```

Figure 5-2 shows the output.

Figure 5-2. *An IconButton*

You could think of a Button as the base class for all of the other buttons. It isn't really, but it wouldn't hurt for you to think of all of the others as a Button with some specialties. For instance, these are all widgets that are specialized types of buttons.

TextButton	TextButton
ElevatedButton	ElevatedButton
IconButton	🗑
FloatingActionButton	FAB
SegmentedButton	Option 1 | Option 2 | Option 3
CupertinoButton	CupertinoButton

Let's take a closer look at them.

71

ElevatedButton

This one is a button that appears like it's floating above the page:

```
ElevatedButton(
  onPressed: () => {},
  child: const Text("ElevatedButton"),
),
```

TextButton and IconButton

These are kind of the anti-ElevatedButton. They just appear completely flat. They are subtle, having simple text or an icon that don't scream to be pressed, like an UNDO button or BACK button.

```
IconButton(
  icon: const Icon(Icons.delete),
  onPressed: () => {},
),
TextButton(
  onPressed: () => {},
  child: const Text("TextButton"),
),
```

FloatingActionButton (FAB)

This is that button you often see in the lower right of the screen. It is usually rounded and is an unmistakable hint to the user on how to progress to the next step in the workflow (Figure 5-3).

Figure 5-3. *Floating action button*

In Flutter, FABs are one of the three main parts of a scaffold. You'll usually see it included sort of like this:

```
Widget build(BuildContext context) {
  return Scaffold(
    appBar: ...,
    body: ...,
    floatingActionButton: FloatingActionButton(
      child: const Icon(Icons.help),
      onPressed: (){},
    ),
  );
}
```

SegmentedButton

This is a group of buttons treated as one unit. One thing can be chosen or multiple can.

```
SegmentedButton(
  emptySelectionAllowed: true,
  multiSelectionEnabled: true,
  selected: selectedValue, // The currently selected value(s)
  onSelectionChanged: (value) =>
      setState(() => selectedValue = value),
```

```
  segments: const [
    ButtonSegment(label: Text('Option 1'), value: 'option1'),
    ButtonSegment(label: Text('Option 2'), value: 'option2'),
    ButtonSegment(label: Text('Option 3'), value: 'option3'),
  ],
),
```

CupertinoButton

An iOS-style button. Looks great on iPhones, but it is kind of strange to have an iOS feel on an Android device. If you use it, you probably intend to wrap it in a CupertinoApp instead of a MaterialApp like the others in this chapter. If you do, make sure you add this to the top of your dart file:

```
import 'package:flutter/cupertino.dart';
```

Dismissible

Buttons are all created for one purpose: to respond to a press. Similarly, a Dismissible is created for one purpose: to respond to a swipe. To use it, you'll usually build a widget and wrap it with a Dismissible. When you do, that widget can then respond to the swipe gesture:

```
Dismissible(
  // Give it a blue background if swiped right and
  // a red background if swiped left
  background: Container(color: Colors.blue),
  secondaryBackground: Container(color: Colors.red),
  onDismissed: (direction) => print("You swiped $direction"),
  child: SomeWidget(),
);
```

Note that as the name suggests, this is used to dismiss a widget, removing it from the view as you "swipe it away." But what if I want to swipe it but not dismiss it? This calls for a custom gesture.

Custom Gestures for Your Custom Widgets

Why does the dismissible understand the swipe gesture? Why do the buttons understand the onPressed gesture? Because the developers wrote them in. Your custom widgets will need to have gestures programmed as well. But since *you're* the one writing them, you get to create your own gestures. And you can create gestures that are way more interesting than a simple press. You can have your widget respond to swipes, long presses, double-presses, and pinch-to-zoom.

Tap	a.k.a. press. Includes double-tapping (tap-tap)
LongPress	Pressing on the screen for a longer time – like a second or two
Scale	a.k.a. pinching or unpinching, when you separate your fingers
Drag	a.k.a. swiping

Note   There's also a Pan, which is similar enough to a Drag that we're omitting for simplicity.

Responding to custom gestures will require these steps:

1. Decide on your gestures and behaviors.

2. Create your custom widget as normal.

3. Add a GestureDetector widget.

4. Associate your gesture with its behavior.

Step 1: Decide on Your Gestures and Behaviors

This step is simple. Your UX expert might have already done it by the time you get ahold of the design. You simply list out the gestures you want to respond to and what they should do when that gesture is detected.

We'll work through an example. Say our user sees a list of people and has to choose the ones they like and the ones they don't. Let's have the user swipe right on each thing they like and swipe left on the ones they don't. And let's say that occasionally the user will want to add a new person between two others. We'll have them separate the two people with their fingers – kind of like making room between them for the new item. And lastly maybe we'll have the user long press to delete the person.

Gesture	Action
Swipe right	Add them to the *nice* list
Swipe left	Add them to the *naughty* list
Pinch (actually reverse-pinch)	Insert a new person
Long press	Delete that person

Step 2: Create Your Custom Widget

Write the Dart code like we've learned in our past chapters. Here's a list of people:

```
class ManagePeople extends StatelessWidget {
  List<Map> fetchPeople() {
    return [
      {"first":"Kevin", "last":"Malone"},
      {"first":"Kelly", "last":"Kapoor"},
      {"first":"Creed", "last":"Bratton"},
```

```
      {"first":"Dwight", "last":"Schrute"},
      {"first":"Andy", "last":"Bernard"},
      {"first":"Pam", "last":"Beasley"},
      {"first":"Jim", "last":"Halpert"},
      {"first":"Robert", "last":"California"},
      {"first":"David", "last":"Wallace"},
      {"first":"Ryan", "last":"Howard"},
    ];
  }
  @override
  Widget build(BuildContext context) {
    var _peopleObjects = fetchPeople();
    return ListView(
      children: _peopleObjects.map((person) =>
        Person(person:person)).toList(),
    );
  }
}
```

Step 3: Add a GestureDetector widget

The GestureDetector widget is different to most UX widgets – you can't
see it. You either wrap a GestureDetector around some widget or nest it
in the child property; it's flexible. Either way, it detects and handles the
gestures for that other widget. Since you can't see it, it's not bloated with
any properties besides child or methods other than build, just what you'd
expect. The events are where the action is!

Here, we're wrapping each Person in a GestureDetector:

```
return ListView(
  children: _peopleObjects
    .map((person) =>
```

```
    GestureDetector(child: Person(person: person))
  ).toList(),
);
```

Step 4: Associate Your Gesture with Its Behavior

Last step. For each event that you designed in step 1, assign a method.
Now GestureDetector supports tons of events[1] so they get really confusing.
We've boiled them down to the most useful ones here.

Gesture	Event(s) to use
Tap (press)	onTap
Double-tap	onDoubleTap
Long press	onLongPress
Side-to-side swipe	onHorizontalDragUpdate, Start, End
Up-and-down swipe	onVerticalDragUpdate, Start, End
Diagonal swipe	onPanUpdate, Start, End
Pinch	onScaleUpdate, Start, End

Example 1: Reacting to a Long Press

A long press (Figure 5-4) will ignore simple taps but will fire when the user
presses for an extended time – like a second or two. Let's say our UX people
decided that a long press will signal that our user wants to delete a user.

---

[1] In addition to the events we've listed, many of these gestures have advanced
events for *Start, *End, *Cancel, *Up, and/or a *Down. These are a lot to take
in but can be useful, so go here to read up on all of them: http://bit.ly/
FlutterGestures

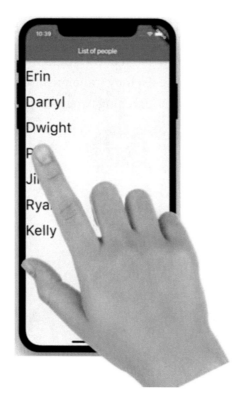

Figure 5-4. *A long press*

To make this happen, we'll add the onLongPress event handler:

```
GestureDetector(
  child: Person(person: person),
  onLongPress: () {
    _people.remove(person);
    print("Deleted ${person['first']}");
  },
);
```

Example 2: Pinching to Add a New Item

Let's say our UX expert suggested that users would want to add items to the list and specify where in the list they want it inserted. To communicate that, they will open the list by unpinching two items (Figure 5-5).

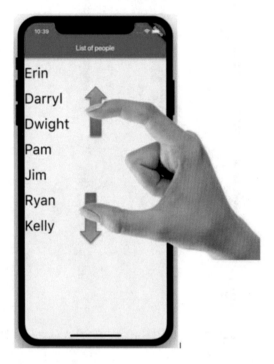

Figure 5-5. *Pinching*

We want to detect if the user was pinching in or pinching out. A normal pinch in should be ignored. But a pinch out – where they spread their fingers out – means we're adding a new person. Note that some event handlers receive in an event object. This object holds information about that particular event. In the case of a scale/pinch, it holds a property called scale. If scale is greater than 1.0, this is a pinch out. Let's say that if the user pinches out twice the normal scale, we'll assume they're wanting to add a new person to the list:

```
onScaleUpdate: (e) {
  if (e.scale > 2.0)
    addPerson(context);
},
```

Example 3: Swiping Left or Right

Now our UX team has decided that if the user swipes right on a person in our list, we should add them to the "nice" list, and if the user swipes left, we'll add them to the "naughty" list (Figure 5-6).

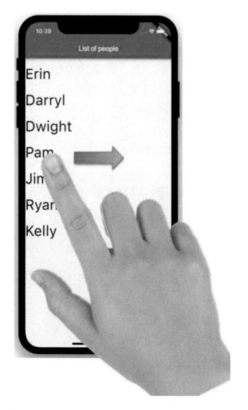

Figure 5-6. *Swiping*

To detect a swipe, we'd look for a drag or a pan. A pan is called for when we expect the user to be able to swipe *diagonally*. HorizontalDrags are only for left and right; it ignores Y-direction. VerticalDrags are only for up and down; it ignores any change in the X-direction. Since we only really care about left swipe or right swipe, we'll zero in on a HorizontalDrag gesture.

Our app can respond to any old swipe by using the onHorizontalDragEnd event. In this case, we also care about the direction of the swipe; was it left to right or right to left? So we have to look at the event object in each case. At the drag start, we save the X-position of where the user's finger was. Then with every pixel move, the drag update event captures the current X-location. Finally, on drag end, we do a simple calculation; if the end X-position is greater, we know it was a swipe right. Otherwise, it was a swipe left:

```
double swipeStartX = 0;
String swipeDirection = "";
return GestureDetector(
  child: Person(person: person),
  onHorizontalDragStart: (e) {
    swipeStartX = e.globalPosition.dx;
  },
  onHorizontalDragUpdate: (e) {
    swipeDirection =
      (e.globalPosition.dx > swipeStartX) ? "Right" : "Left";
  },
  onHorizontalDragEnd: (e) {
    if (_swipeDirection == "Right")
      updatePerson(person, status: "nice");
    else
      updatePerson(person, status: "naughty");
  },
);
```

Conclusion

Flutter gestures are intuitive. They work like the average developer would expect them to, making it easy for us to code and easy for our users to use. When triggered, all events will run on a separate thread so it is totally okay to have them return an Async<> object. Therefore, feel free to mark your event handling functions as async and fill them full of awaits.[2]

---

[2] For more information on Futures, async, and await, take a look at Appendix B, "Futures, Async, and Await."

CHAPTER 6

Navigation and Routing

All apps have the concept of *moving* from one screen to another. The user clicks the cart button, and we go to the card scene. The user clicks "continue shopping" button, and we get to browse for more products to buy. Some app developers call it routing. Others call it navigation. Whatever you want to call it, this is one area that Flutter makes easy because there are only four ways of navigating:

- Stacks – Each widget is full screen. The user taps buttons to go through a predefined workflow. History is maintained, and they can travel back by hitting a back button.

- Drawers – Most of the screen shows a widget, but on the left edge, a drawer is peeking out at the user. When they press it or swipe it right, it slides out revealing a menu of choices. Pressing one changes the widget in the main part of the screen.

- Tabs – Some room is reserved for a set of tabs at the top or the bottom of the screen. When you press on a tab, we show the widget that corresponds to that tab.

© Rap Payne 2024
R. Payne, *Flutter App Development*, https://doi.org/10.1007/979-8-8688-0485-4_6

- Dialogs – While these aren't technically part of navigation, they are a way to see another widget, so we'll allow it. Dialogs are modal (a.k.a. pop-up windows) that stay until the user dismisses them.

Each of these methods depends on your app having a MaterialWidget as its ancestor. Let's drill into these methods starting with stack navigation.

Stack Navigation

If you're an experienced developer, you're familiar with queues and stacks. If not, let me explain briefly. Let's say you work in a kitchen. As plates are cleaned, they're stacked, right? Each plate is put on the top of the stack. This is called *pushing* onto the stack. When it is time to serve some food, you naturally take the last plate added, the one on top of the stack. This is called *popping* off the top of the stack.

Flutter's navigation works with stacks. When you want to send the user to a new scene, you will push() a widget on the top of the stack and the user sees that widget. Each time you push(), you're making the stack of scenes taller and taller. When you are ready for them to go back to where they were before, you'll pop() the last scene off the top of the stack, and what is revealed? The previous scene.

With Flutter's stack, you'll typically predefine the scenes (a.k.a. routes) and give each a name. This must be done at the MaterialApp level like so:

```
Widget build(BuildContext context) {
  return MaterialApp(
    title: 'Shopping App',
    initialRoute: '/',
    routes: {
      '/': (ctx) => LandingScene(),
      '/browse': (ctx) => Browse(),
```

```
    '/product': (ctx) => ViewProduct(),
    '/checkout: (ctx) => Checkout(),
  },
);
}
```

Note that with routing, we no longer use the home property. Instead, use the intialRoute property.

Tip   If your initialRoute is "/", you can omit it altogether and Flutter assumes it is "/".

Navigating Forward and Back

To navigate between scenes, you'll use Navigator.pushNamed(context, route) and Navigator.pop(context).

To push a user to another route:

```
RaisedButton(
  child: const Text('Check out'),
  onPressed: () => Navigator.pushNamed(context, '/checkout),
),
```

Once they're finished and want to go back:

```
RaisedButton(
  child: const Text('Go back'),
  onPressed: () => Navigator.pop(context),
),
```

But wait, there's more! Notice that if you have a Scaffold, a back arrow is automatically added to the appBar (Figure 6-1). When tapped, it works to go back. And if your user is on Android, the ubiquitous Android back button works also (Figure 6-2).

Figure 6-1. *The back arrow in the appBar*

Figure 6-2. *The Android back button works with stacks*

Using Anonymous Routes

With named routes, your routing scheme is self-documenting. When your teammates want to review the scene-level widgets, they merely go to the MaterialApp and find the routes. Voila! There are the places you can go.

There is another flavor of routing that doesn't use a predefined routing table in your MaterialApp. Instead, you generate the route on the fly. We call this anonymous routing because there's no name. Anonymous routing is more ad hoc and more flexible but it's also more unpredictable for your teammates.

At any time, you can

```
Navigator.push(
 context,
 MaterialPageRoute<void>(builder:
  (BuildContext context) => SecondRoute()
 )
);
```

As you can see, it's quite a bit more complex. But it is popular if you want custom transitions or just don't want predefined routes. With this, you can navigate to any widget whether it is in the named route listing or not.

Get Result After a Scene Is Closed

With stack navigation, every pop() returns to its caller. Therefore, it is possible to return a value from each scene. This isn't extremely common, but it can be super useful when you're moving the user through a workflow. Let's say you have a section of your app that maintains a person object. The person object is defined in MyPersonWidget, and we provide one button to modify the login credentials, another to modify the phone number, and yet another to modify the X/Twitter handle. When the user taps each button, we might push() them to a route where they change the data. If so, we'll need to return that changed data to the MyPersonWidget when we pop(). In this case, we will push() a little differently; we'll have a variable to receive the returned value:

```
// The 'async' is needed here because we are 'await'ing below.
onPressed:  () async {
  _person.xHandle =
          await Navigator.pushNamed(context, '/xHandle');
},
```

Note   The *await* keyword implies that pushNamed() returns a Future. Also note that any value returned from this route will be assigned to _person.xHandle.

So how does this value get returned from the XWidget? In the pop() of course!

```
Navigator.pop<String>(context, xHandle);
```

Navigator.pop() is overloaded. If you add a second parameter, it will be returned to the widget that called push() in the first place. In the preceding example, xHandle will be returned.

Apps that are shallow work great with push() and pop(). But your app may have a deep navigation tree with lots of choices. Apps like that aren't usually best served by having umpteen buttons to push() and pop(). Instead, they should have a navigation menu. Flutter provides us with two types. Simpler apps can have tabs. More complex apps will have drawers. Let's look at drawers next.

Drawer Navigation

Drawers are great when we have a lot of navigation choices – too many choices to fit in a tab. In a lot of responsive websites, you'll see a menu across the top of the page with links to other pages on the site. Then when the site is viewed on a small device or even a narrow browser, that menu is replaced by a hamburger menu that, when clicked, will drop down a menu filled with the same choices. Basically, this is the site responding to limited screen real estate, providing menu choices that are hidden until the user asks for them.

Since most phones already have limited screen real estate, you may opt to put your menu choices in a drawer that doesn't gobble up that precious screen real estate until the user is ready to see them (Figure 6-3). They will hit the now-familiar hamburger menu (that icon with three lines) and the choices slide out from the left (Figure 6-4). When the user chooses one, we'll Navigator.push() them to a new route.

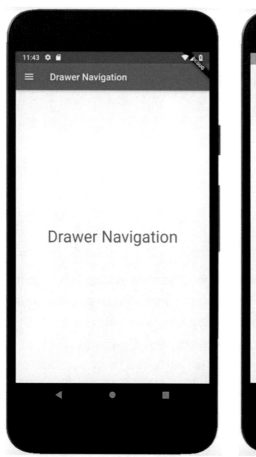

Figure 6-3. *A scene with the drawer closed*

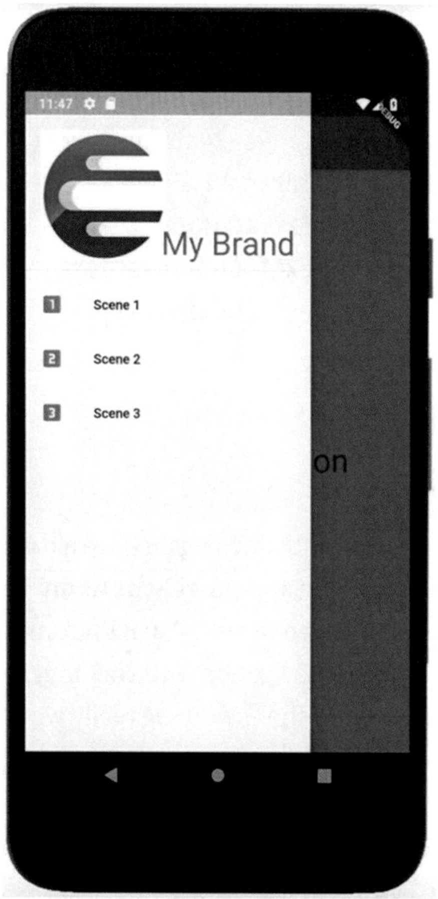

Figure 6-4. *A scene with the drawer open*

The Drawer Widget

You'll need a NavigationDrawer widget, a built-in Flutter widget that has the ability to slide out, slide in, and contain menu choices. When you use a drawer, you always include it in a Scaffold's drawer property, like this:

```
Widget build(BuildContext context) {
  return Scaffold(
    body: SomeFullPageWidget(),
    drawer: NavigationDrawer(child: Column(
      children: <Widget>[
        Text('Option 1'),
        Text('Option 2'),
        Text('Option 3'),
      ],
    ),),),
  );
}
```

Notice that when you have a drawer in your Scaffold, its hamburger icon replaces the appBar's back button. You can't see both buttons simultaneously unless you create your own buttons manually. So while drawer navigation and stack navigation *can* work together, it can be kind of awkward. One example of them working really well together is to have a Drawer at the topmost level, and then use stack navigation at all levels below that.

Tip   Do you want a consistent drawer to be available across your entire app? If so, we generally put a Scaffold on every scene and include the drawer in it. Therefore, it is best to put your Drawer in its own widget and include it.

```
return Scaffold(
    appBar: AppBar(
      title: const Text('Drawer Navigation'),
    ),
  body: const Text('DrawerNavigation'),
  drawer: MyDrawer(),
);
```

Filling the Drawer

Adding the drawer is easy. The trick is getting entries into the drawer and then making them navigate to another widget. Note that Drawer has a *child* property that accepts a single widget. To get multiple children in your drawer, you will use a widget that supports them such as Column (doesn't scroll) or ListView (scrolls).

Whichever you choose, you'll want to put something that is tappable because to navigate, you're going to call Navigator.push() or Navigator.pushNamed() just like you did with stack navigation.

Tip   There's a cool widget called a DrawerHeader that is built to take up a large area at the top of the drawer. It is great for putting your logo or other branding information to sort of remind the user what app they are in. It is cosmetic only but it really does look cool.

Here's the code all together. It's the code that generated the screenshot in Figure 6-4.

```
return Drawer(
 child: ListView(
  children: [
    DrawerHeader(
      child: Stack(
        children: [
          Image.asset('lib/assets/Logo.jpg'),
          Container(
              alignment: Alignment.bottomRight,
              child: Text('My Brand')),
        ],
      ),
    ),
```

```
  ListTile(
    leading: const Icon(Icons.looks_one),
    title: const Text('Widget 1'),
    onTap: () => Navigator.pushNamed(context, '/widget1')
  ),
  ListTile(
    leading: const Icon(Icons.looks_two),
    title: const Text('Widget 2'),
    onTap: () => Navigator.pushNamed(context, '/widget2')
  ),
  ListTile(
    leading: const Icon(Icons.looks_3),
    title: const Text('Widget 3'),
    onTap: () => Navigator.pushNamed(context, '/widget3')
  ),
 ],
 ),
);
```

Drawer navigation is great and all, but UX experts have a few problems with it. They claim[1] that it drastically reduces the usability of apps, making your app less discoverable and more difficult. They say the problem is that the options are hidden until the user asks for them. Their objection could be resolved with an affordance that is always visible. Speaking of which ...

---

[1] http://bit.ly/HamburgerNav

Tab Navigation

As you would imagine, a tab system matches N tabs with N widgets. When the user presses tab 1, they see widget 1 and so forth (Figure 6-5). The matching is done with a DefaultTabController, a TabBar widget with Tabs, and a TabBarView widget.

Figure 6-5. *A TabBar with the second tab chosen*

Figure 6-6. *Same TabBar with the fourth tab chosen*

Tip   While there's no hard upper limit on the number of tabs you can have, your app will get frustratingly hard to use if you put too many on the TabBar. It's just too tough to press those tiny, tiny tabs. If you're desperate, you can set isScrollable to true and let the user know they can swipe left to scroll the tab list.

DefaultTabController

The DefaultTabController is the least obvious part. Just know that you have to have one or you get the error in Figure 6-7.

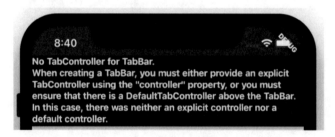

Figure 6-7.   *When you forget a TabController*

The easiest way to create one is to wrap everything in a DefaultTabController() with a length property. Problem solved. This part is pretty simple – so simple you may wonder why Flutter doesn't create one implicitly for you. If you were thinking that, you wouldn't be wrong:

```
Widget build(BuildContext context) {
  return DefaultTabController(
    length: 5,
    child: Scaffold(
    ...
  );
}
```

TabBarView

Next you'll want to add a TabBarView widget. This holds the widgets that will eventually be shown when the user presses a tab, defining *where* they will be shown. Usually this is the entire rest of the screen, but you have the opportunity to put widgets above the TabBarView or below it or really anywhere around it. You should provide the same number of widgets as the length property of the DefaultTabController (duh):

```
child: Scaffold(
 ...
 body: TabBarView(
  children: <Widget>[
    WidgetA(),
    WidgetB(),
    WidgetC(),
    WidgetD(),
    WidgetE(),
  ],
 ),
```

TabBar and Tabs

Lastly, we define the tabs themselves. Tabs can either hold text or an icon or both. Here's a TabBar with five tabs, each having just an icon:

```
child: Scaffold(
 appBar: AppBar(
  title: const Text('Tab Navigation Demo'),
  bottom: const TabBar(
    tabs: [
      Tab(icon: Icon(Icons.looks_one)),
      Tab(icon: Icon(Icons.looks_two)),
```

```
    Tab(icon: Icon(Icons.looks_3)),
    Tab(icon: Icon(Icons.looks_4)),
    Tab(icon: Icon(Icons.looks_5)),
   ],
 ),
 ),
 ...
```

To add text to the Tab(), provide a child property: Tab(child: Text('Choice 1')).

Caution   There's a one-to-one correspondence between each tab and each TabBarView child; they are matched positionally. You must have the same number of tabs as you do widgets inside the TabBarView and in the same order.

TabBar at the Bottom

Note that previously we chose to put the TabBar in the appBar, which of course appears at the top of the screen. But sometimes your design calls for the tabs to appear at the bottom of the screen. That's easy because the Scaffold has a property called bottomNavigationBar, and it is built to hold a TabBar:

```
child: Scaffold(
  ...
bottomNavigationBar: const TabBar(
  tabs: [
    Tab(icon: Icon(Icons.looks_one)),
    Tab(icon: Icon(Icons.looks_two)),
```

```
      Tab(icon: Icon(Icons.looks_3)),
      Tab(icon: Icon(Icons.looks_4)),
      Tab(icon: Icon(Icons.looks_5)),
    ],
  ),
  ),
```

Figure 6-8. *TabBar at the bottom*

Note   The TabBar has the normal appearance of light text on a dark background. Thus, when you place the TabBar on top of a light background, it may be difficult to see the text (light on light). To fix this, wrap your TabBar in a Material widget with a darker background color.

The Dialog Widget

Our last navigation category is arguably not a navigation category at all – dialogs. In one sense, you're showing another widget so ... navigation? But in another sense, you're basically showing a pop-up so ... not navigation. ‾_(ツ)_/‾

Either way, dialogs are a common thing and we should cover them. Since they don't fit well anywhere else in the book, let's pretend for the moment that they are a navigation topic. Hey, work with me here.

showDialog( ) and AlertDialog

showDialog() is a built-in Flutter method. You must supply a context and a builder method that returns a Widget, usually either SimpleDialog or AlertDialog. The AlertDialog has an *actions* parameter – a List of (typically) FlatButtons that let the user dismiss the dialog (Figure 6-9).

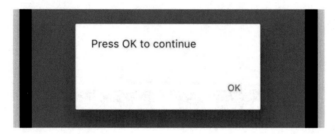

Figure 6-9. *A simple AlertDialog*

```
ElevatedButton(
  child: const Text('I am a button. Press me'),
  onPressed: () => showDialog<void>(
    context: context,
    builder: (BuildContext context) {
      return AlertDialog(
        content: const Text('Press OK to continue'),
        actions: <Widget>[
          TextButton(
            child: const Text('OK'),
            onPressed: () => Navigator.pop(context)),
        ],
      );
    },
  ),
),
```

This looks more complex than it needs to be. And this is the simplest form! It gets more complex if you want to give the user choices.

100

Responses with a Dialog

showDialog() returns a Future<T> which means that you can have it return a value to its caller. Let's pretend you want the user to respond with yes or no (Figure 6-10).

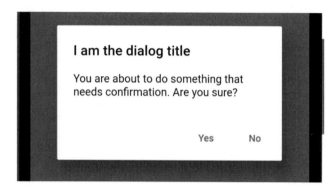

Figure 6-10. *AlertDialog that returns a value*

You might create the dialog and handle the response like this:

```
ElevatedButton(
 child: const Text('Get a response'),
 onPressed: () async {
  // The builder returns the user's choice here.
  // Since it is a Future<String>, we 'await' it to
  // convert it to a String
  String response = await showDialog<String>(
    context: context,
    builder: (BuildContext context) {
      return AlertDialog(
        content: const Text('Are you sure?'),
        actions: <Widget>[
          TextButton(
              child: const Text('Yes'),
```

```
            // Return "Yes" when dismissed.
            onPressed: () => Navigator.pop(context, 'Yes')),
         TextButton(
            child: const Text('No'),
            // Return "No" when dismissed.
            onPressed: () => Navigator.pop(context, 'No')),
      ],
    );
  },
);
// Do things with the response that we 'await'ed above.
print(response);
},
),
```

Tip   As the name suggests, the SimpleDialog widget is a simpler version of the AlertDialog. It doesn't have actions because it's dismissed by tapping anywhere. It has fewer constructor parameters like titleTextStyle, contentTextStyle, and the like. Use it mainly if you don't need the user to respond to the prompt but simply to inform.

Navigation Methods Can Be Combined

While you can stack navigate to a widget with a drawer and from there to a widget with a tab, you should be careful. The methods are not incompatible, but, boy, they can get complex when mixed! Think about it; if you stack navigate via push() to a widget with a drawer, the back button in the appBar is no longer available. Android has a soft back button at the bottom, but iOS does not. So the user is now stuck with no way to return.

Another example, a TabBarView has widgets, but these are hosted so to speak so they should have no Scaffold. If you tried to navigate to that same widget using either of the other two methods, you have no way to get back … no drawer to show and no back button to tap. Again, the user is stuck.

We recommend sticking to just two different types and keeping the levels consistent. For example, it is pretty common to have a tabbed navigation experience for the user, and within each tab, you'll work with stack navigation. But get much more complex than that and you may get your hands full.

CHAPTER 7

Managing State

We kind of telegraphed this topic since the first chapter because we've been writing classes that extend a StatelessWidget. Now if Flutter has a State**less**Widget, then you'd think it also has a State**ful**Widget. And you'd be right.

But what exactly is a StatefulWidget? How does it differ from a stateless one? When do we choose one vs. the other? What is the structure of a StatefulWidget? Are there rules for using one? If the data changes, how do you re-render it? Good questions, right? Well, be patient young Jedi and we'll answer all of those and more in this chapter.

Caution   This chapter isn't for the faint-hearted. In it, we're introducing some mind-bending concepts. Not that you can't handle it! We're just giving you a heads up so that when you encounter some of these deeper concepts and code, you don't get discouraged. Just be ready is all.

What Is State?

State is widget data whose change requires a re-render.

—Rap Payne ;-)

R. Payne, *Flutter App Development*, https://doi.org/10.1007/979-8-8688-0485-4_7

StatelessWidgets might have data, but that data either doesn't change while the widget is alive or doesn't change how the screen looks. Sure, this data may change when Flutter destroys and recreates the widget, but that doesn't count. To be state, it must change while the widget is active.

Flutter gives us certain widgets that are state*ful* out of the box.

- AppBar
- BottomNavigationBar
- Checkbox
- DefaultTabController
- Dismissible
- DrawerController
- DropdownButton
- EditableText
- Form
- FormField
- GlowingOverscrollIndicator
- Image
- InputDecorator
- MonthPicker
- Navigator
- ProgressIndicator
- Radio
- RefreshIndicator
- Scaffold
- Scrollbar
- Slider
- Switch
- TextField
- YearPicker

… and many more. These all have internal data that must be maintained and monitored so that as it changes, Flutter re-renders the widget to display said change to the screen. Is that difficult to follow? Let's take a simple example: a TextField widget.

Yes, we're talking about the built-in widget that behaves like a textbox; the end user types characters into it. You realize of course that as the user types, the widget is keeping track of and displaying the stuff they're typing. That, my friend, is state – data that changes and is displayed live.

That's great and all, but how do we write our own StatefulWidgets? Read on!

The Shape of a StatefulWidget

Here's how every StatefulWidget looks:

```
class Foo extends StatefulWidget {
  @override
  State<Foo> createState() => _FooState();
}
class _FooState extends State<Foo> {
  //Private variables here are considered the 'state'
  @override
  Widget build(BuildContext context) {
    return someWidget;
  }
}
```

Note   There are two classes: the widget class and a state class!

Any stateful widget appears complex at first, but once you get accustomed to its structure, it becomes second nature. We traditionally write both classes in a single Dart file. The widget class inherits from StatefulWidget and is public because it is the thing that will be placed in other widgets.

The state class is always private because the current widget is the only thing that will ever see this class. The state class is responsible to ...

1. Define and maintain the state data.

2. Define the build() method – It knows how to draw the widget on screen.

3. Define any callback functions needed for data gathering or event handling.

107

What does that leave for the widget class? Not much. The widget class just kind of gets out of the way.

So then why separate them? There are two reasons. First, the single responsibility principle[1] (the SRP) suggests that we should have one thing responsible for drawing the widget and another thing responsible for dealing with data. That's just good software design. Other frameworks suggest that you separate UI from state management, but most don't enforce it. Flutter does.

Second is performance. Redrawing takes time. Recalculating state takes time. When we separate them like this, we are giving Flutter a chance to handle these two things independently. Sometimes a redraw doesn't need to happen just because state changes. So we save the cycles of redrawing.

Also, when we redraw, Flutter creates and draws a whole new widget. The old widget in memory is no longer needed so it is dereferenced and eventually garbage collected. That's awesome but state is still needed. If Flutter retains that old state object, it can be reused instead of being garbage collected and recreated. By separating these objects, Flutter decouples them so they can each be handled in its own most efficient way. It's a brilliant design!

The Most Important Rule About State!

All changes to state data must be made ...

1. In the state class

2. Inside a function call to setState():

---

[1] https://en.wikipedia.org/wiki/Single_responsibility_principle

```
setState(() {
  // Make all changes to state variables here...
  _value = 42; // <-- ... Like this
});
```

setState() takes a function which is run … uh … soon. The Flutter subsystem batches changes and runs them all at a time that it decides is optimal. This is extremely efficient because, among other reasons, it will reduce the number of screen redraws.

setState() not only sets the variables in the most efficient and controlled way, but it always forces a re-render of this widget to occur. It invokes build() behind the scenes. The end result: when you change a value, the widget redraws itself and your user sees the new version. Note that if this widget has subwidgets inside of it (aka *inner* widgets), they'll be in the build() method, so a call to setState() actually redraws **everything** in this widget including all of its subtrees.

If this causes you to panic for a second, please remember that Flutter uses a virtual widget tree, so even though we are telling it to draw everything, it is smart enough to know what parts of the screen don't need a refresh and it only technically redraws those parts that do need it. It is superefficient!

Passing State Down

Okay, you got me. Technically, you can't pass state from a host widget into an inner widget because state only exists *within* a widget. But we definitely want to pass data down. That data may be stateful data in the host widget, and it may be moved to state in the inner widget.

But this is nothing new. We did it with Stateless Widgets. As a reminder, you simply declare class-scoped final variables and supply their initial values in constructor parameters.

But how is the passed value visible in the State class? Flutter provides us an object called *widget* which represents the StatefulWidget. In other words, if there is a variable called "x" in the StatefulWidget, it is visible in the State class as "widget.x":

```
class Foo extends StatefulWidget {
 // Value passed in from its host
 Foo({required this.passedIn, super.key});
 final String passedIn;
 State<Foo> createState() => _FooState();
}
class _FooState extends State<Foo> {
  @override
  Widget build(BuildContext context) {
    return Text(widget.passedIn,); // <-- See? "widget."!
  }
}
```

Now that we know how to pass data down from host widget to inner widget, let's go the other way and see how to pass data back up from the inner widget to the host.

Lifting State Back Up

Aaaaand you got me again. You can't pass state. But it gets worse. With Flutter, you can't pass anything *up*.

Flutter has one-way data flow. Period. Data can only flow down from a host widget to an inner widget. We've been doing this for, what, about 200 pages now? But sometimes we need data to flow from an inner back up to a host.

For instance, let's say we have a Login widget with username/password TextFields and a submit button. We'd place this Login in other widgets provided that the user is not already logged in. The business logic to log in must be in the Login widget itself. But when they successfully log in, we really need to let the host widget – or even all widgets – know the user is now authenticated. The token needs to be passed back up. But how do we do that when we can't pass data (state) up to a host?

Here's the trick. Don't pass the data *up*. Pass the handler method *down*! In Dart, functions are first-class objects. This means that their references can be passed around like data. This also means that you can pass a function from a host widget down into inner widgets. Now that the inner widget has a handle to this function, it can invoke it as if it were its own. But of course when the inner widget invokes it, if it passes a value into that function, the value is seen in the host where the function was originally defined.

This technique is called *lifting state up* (Figure 7-1).

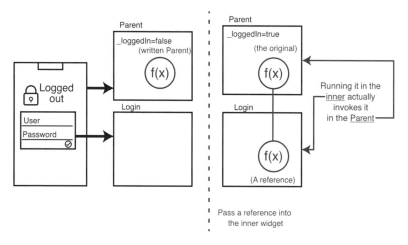

Figure 7-1. *Lifting the state up*

An Example of State Management

We should probably look at some code to solidify these concepts. Let's say we have an app that allows its user to create a color by adjusting red, green, and blue values on three sliders. These will mix the colors and show it in a bigger circle (Figure 7-2).

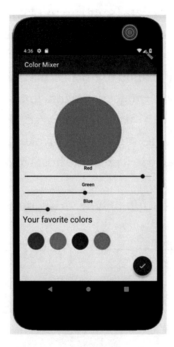

Figure 7-2. *An example Stateful Widget*

Clearly the big circle needs to redraw as slider data changes. Changing data that requires a redraw is state! While we technically could have all of this in one big widget called ColorMixer, we've learned in this book to decompose large widgets into smaller, more specialized ones. Let's extract the ColorCircle and use it for the big circle at the top and also for the favorite colors at the bottom. And since we've got three sliders with labels, all doing the same thing, we should probably extract the slider/label also into a ColorValueChanger. So how about the layout in Figure 7-3?

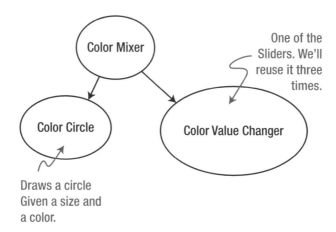

Figure 7-3. *How we might lay out the widget tree*

The ColorMixer must be stateful:

```dart
import 'package:flutter/material.dart';
import 'color_circle.dart';
import 'color_value_changer.dart';

// The stateful widget
class ColorMixer extends StatefulWidget {
 const ColorMixer({super.key});
 @override
 State<ColorMixer> createState() => _ColorMixerState();
}

// The state class
class _ColorMixerState extends State<ColorMixer> {
 // These three variables are the 'state' of the widget
 int _redColor = 0;
 int _blueColor = 0;
 int _greenColor = 0;
```

113

```
@override
Widget build(BuildContext context) {
 return Column(
  children: <Widget>[
   // This widget uses the variables (aka state)
   ColorCircle(
    color: Color.fromRGBO(
    _redColor, _greenColor, _blueColor, 1),
     radius: 200,
   ),
   // These three pass the _setColor function down so that
   // the state *here* can be changed at lower levels. This
   // is called "lifting state up".
   ColorValueChanger(property: "Red", value: _redColor,
    changeColorValue: _setColor),
   ColorValueChanger(property:"Green",value:_greenColor,
    changeColorValue:_setColor),
   ColorValueChanger(property: "Blue",value:_blueColor,
    changeColorValue: _setColor),
  ],
 );
}

void _setColor(String property, int value) {
 setState(() {
  _redColor = (property == "Red") ? value : _redColor;
  _greenColor = (property == "Green") ? value : _greenColor;
  _blueColor = (property == "Blue") ? value : _blueColor;
 });
}
}
```

Don't miss this: we're passing 100% of what ColorCircle needs into it –
a color and a size. Neither of those change inside ColorCircle, so it can be
stateless. If ColorMixer's state changes, we simply call setState(), thereby
re-rendering it and consequently all instances of its child, ColorCircle. Do
you see it? The child(ren) ColorCircle can be stateless because its state*ful*
parent ColorMixer passes state variables down!

In the same manner, we pass an initial value into each
ColorValueChanger, and we pass a reference to the _setColor method.
Remember, passing a function down makes it available and therefore
executable in the child widget. Although the child widget executes it, the
function actually exists in the parent widget!

Here's how it would look in the inner ColorValueChanger widget:

```
import 'package:flutter/material.dart';
class ColorValueChanger extends StatefulWidget {
 // Value passed in from its host
 const ColorValueChanger({
   required this.property,
   required this.value,
   required this.changeColorValue, super.key});
 final String property;
 final int value;
 final Function changeColorValue; //<-- Passed in!

 @override
 State<ColorValueChanger> createState() =>
  _ColorValueChangerState();
}

class _ColorValueChangerState extends State<ColorValueChanger> {
 int _value = 0;
 @override
 Widget build(BuildContext context) {
  _value = widget.value;
```

```
 return Column(
  children: <Widget>[
   Text(widget.property),
   Slider(
    min: O, max: 255,
    value: _value.toDouble(),
    label: widget.property,
    onChanged: _onChanged,
   )
  ],
 );
}

_onChanged(double value) {
 setState(() => _value = value.round());
 // And this is where we call the setter function passed
 // in from the host (parent) widget.
 widget.changeColorValue(widget.property, value.round());
 }
}
```

When Should We Use State?

But you know what? The very best way to avoid complex state is to avoid having state at all. Just about every expert agrees that if you can avoid state altogether, do. But it can be confusing as to when you need state and when you don't.

For example, the label on our color picker is data within the component. Should that be state? No, of course not; it doesn't change. How about a loop counter on a for loop? Nope; it never affects anything in the build() method, so it doesn't need to be put in a setState(). See? State can sometimes be simplified or eliminated.

Figure 7-4 provides a summary of how to decide.

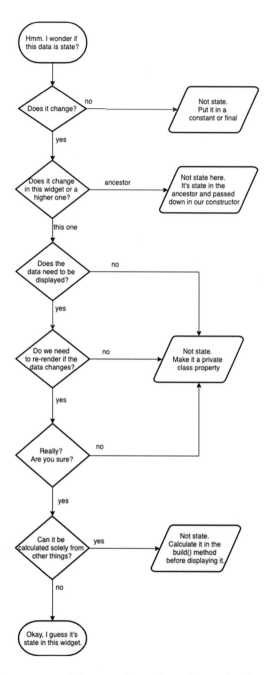

Figure 7-4. *How you might go about deciding whether state should actually be used in a widget*

117

Conclusion

So now you know. State is data that is likely to change and will affect the display somehow. It must be changed inside a setState() method or it will never be seen by the user. It can only exist privately in a StatefulWidget – it is inaccessible by other widgets.

But this poses a major, major problem. If state is truly private, what happens when we need to share data between different widgets? We can pass data down through the constructor, and we can lift it up by passing a function down. But what about between distant relatives? What about sharing tons of complex data? We have a few solutions for you and that's the subject of the next chapter – state management libraries!

CHAPTER 8

State Management Libraries

What we learned in the last chapter would work as advertised even when the widget tree gets infinitely deep. We could continue to lift state up and pass state down forever. But please realize that as your app gets bigger and bigger, state management becomes more and more complex. When it gets too complex, you will be better served by using a more advanced state management pattern. These patterns are not usually easy to learn, but at some point in your app's growth, they become worth the effort to master.

In this chapter, we're going to look at a few patterns, a few widgets, and a few libraries. Then we'll focus in on two libraries: a simple one and the one that is currently the most popular, Riverpod.

The InheritedWidget

This is a relatively simple solution, maybe too simple for most needs. InheritedWidget [1] is a built-in Flutter widget. Essentially, it exposes a small set of variables that are made available to all descendants in its tree. In a sense, it creates pseudo-global variables. They're available everywhere beneath the InheritedWidget but only in a very controlled way. The InheritedWidget defines the variables that need to be shared among all

---

[1] https://docs.flutter.io/flutter/widgets/InheritedWidget-class.html

R. Payne, *Flutter App Development*, https://doi.org/10.1007/979-8-8688-0485-4_8

descendants. Then the descendant widgets are able to query up the chain for the InheritedWidget and access those variables. Several of the other methods (Provider, Redux, Riverpod, etc.) are wrappers around InheritedWidget.

Pros: Simplest of all of the solutions in this chapter.

Cons: And despite that, it is still daunting for many new Flutter users. It is spartan and only appropriate for the most rudimentary application state.

The BLoC Pattern

BLoC, an acronym for business logic components, is neither a library nor a widget. It is a design pattern. The BLoC pattern was originally created to allow the reuse of the code across the Web, mobile applications, and backend. Because it was created at Google, it was natural that the Flutter Community embraced it where it became synonymous with state management, at least for a while.

BLoC involves treating data as streams and altering state reactively. It separates the UI (user interface) from the business logic, making your code more

- Maintainable – Clearer separation of concerns leads to easier code navigation and updates.

- Testable – You can test business logic independently of UI interactions.

- Scalable – Handle complex app states effectively.

BLoC has many different parts:

- StreamControllers that control the streams of data

- StreamTransformers that can process the data as it flows in

- StreamBuilders that run when a new value arrives and render it in the UI

120

Pros: Lots of folks in the community can and will help you. It is a solid, well-vetted pattern.

Cons: BLoC is anything but simple to understand and to write. There is a bloc library that can help, but most people write BLoC components without the library so it is very low-level.

Some Libraries
ScopedModel

ScopedModel[2] is a library "shamelessly borrowed" from the Fuchsia[3] codebase by Brian Egan. (Hey, these are Brian's own words, not mine! He's a humble guy.) ScopedModel creates data models with the ability to register listeners. Each model notifies its listeners when the data has changed so they can update themselves. Clever design.

It is an external third-party package maintained by Brian. It is built on top of InheritedWidget offering a slightly better way to access, update, and mutate the state. It allows you to easily pass a data model from a parent widget down to its descendants and rebuilds all the children that use the model when the model is updated.

Pros: Does its job of separating presentation and data very well. Compared to others in this chapter, it is simpler to understand.

Cons: The code base isn't currently being maintained, probably because developers are leaning on more modern solutions. Some have said that ScopedModel has performance problems for complex apps.

---

[2] https://pub.dartlang.org/packages/scoped_model
[3] https://fuchsia.googlesource.com/

Redux and Hooks

I only include these two libraries for you React devs. Both of these are libraries that emulate the React features of the same name. If you're not coming from the world of React, skip this section. But if you love yourself some React, these may be your simplest options. Heck, you've already mastered the learning curve. flutter_redux[4] was written by Brian Egan who we heard about earlier from ScopedModel, and flutter_hooks[5] was written by Rémi Rousselet of Paris who you'll hear about in a minute from Provider and Riverpod.

Pros: Very performant. Very scalable.

Cons: Very steep learning curves unless you already know React.

Provider

I include Provider here not because you're likely to use it but because you're likely to hear about it, and I don't want you to be tempted. There is a better option. At one point, Provider was the most popular Flutter state management library. But it has been supplanted by a better option: Riverpod (covered in the last section in this chapter).

Pros: A very capable package that is comparatively simple to use.

Cons: Not being actively maintained because of its successor, Riverpod.

Whoa! That's a Lot of Packages!

Confused yet? I don't blame you. These packages all solve the same problem in different ways, some similarly and others using wildly different strategies. No one has any expectations that you'll have anything more

---

[4] https://pub.dartlang.org/packages/flutter_redux
[5] https://pub.dartlang.org/documentation/flutter_hooks

than an awareness that there are tools out there. When you hear someone say something like "Our state is getting messy. Maybe we should take a look at BLoC or ScopedModel," you'll at least know that type of thing they're talking about. Then you can dig into the technologies to see which you might want to use.

But wouldn't it be nice to have an idea of a solution or two that you could actually use? Let's write a little code for two of these state management solutions: the simplest one, raw_state, and the most popular and robust one, flutter_riverpod.

Raw State

raw_state (`https://pub.dev/packages/raw_state`) is ideal for learning Flutter which is why we're including it here. It's also decent for a very simple application and for getting your MVP off the ground. It solves the problem of sharing between widgets by creating a global variable called rawState. As soon as you `flutter pub add raw_state` and then import raw_state, this rawState variable is automatically defined.

```
import 'package:raw_state/raw_state.dart';
```

Then in any widget, you write any number of values to rawState:

```
String foo = "raw_state is stupidly simple";
rawState.set("aString", foo);
rawState.set("aDate", DateTime.now());
rawState.set("aMap", {"foo":"bar","baz":100} );
```

Note   The keys can be any string and the values can be anything – String, double, int, bool, Array, Map, object … whatever.

In any other widget, you can read those values from rawState. Merely call get, passing in the key:

```
String foo = rawState.get("aString");
DateTime someDate = rawState.get<DateTime>("aDate");
Map<String, dynamic> aMap =
    rawState.get<Map<String, dynamic>>("aMap");
```

Tip   The data type (a.k.a. generics) is optional but is a good practice for safety reasons. Note that for the sake of demonstrations, we omitted it in the first but included it for the rest.

---

raw_state is ridiculously simple. Maybe too simple. It lacks lots of protections and any auto-updating capabilities that many of the other libraries have. So let's turn our attention to one last library, Riverpod, written by the aforementioned Rémi Rousselet.

Riverpod

At the time of writing, Riverpod is the go-to state management solution. It is complete and robust and less complicated than some of the libraries above. A winning combination.

Caution   Please don't misunderstand. I didn't say that Riverpod is simple. It's not. So if you're not planning to use Riverpod soon, don't feel bad about skipping to the next chapter. I'm going to lay out the simplest possible steps to use Riverpod just to get you started. But even then, it's daunting.

Here are the six basic steps to use Riverpod.

One-time, up-front preparation:

1. Install flutter_riverpod

2. Wrap your App with a ProviderScope

3. Write a Provider

Then in every widget where needed:

1. Inherit from ConsumerStateWidget

2. Read data with ref.watch()

3. Write data with ref.read()

Let's examine these steps.

1. Install flutter_riverpod

This step is simple. Either add it to your pubspec.yaml and run flutter pub get or run

```
flutter pub add flutter_riverpod
```

2. Wrap Your App with a ProviderScope

Remember that in your main, we call runApp(App()). Merely wrap that app with a ProviderScope that has been imported from flutter_riverpod:

```
void main() => runApp(
 ProviderScope(
  child: App()
 )
);
```

3. Write a Provider

Before we can store values, we will create one provider *for each thing* we want to share. Let's say we allow the user to pick their favorite color in one widget and then read it in the rest. We might create a favColorProvier:

```
final favColorProvider =
          StateProvider<Color>((_) => Colors.red);
```

Obviously, StateProvider is part of Riverpod.

Wait, What Is This *Provider* You Speak Of?

We're done with prep, the steps that are done once and up-front. Before we turn to using Riverpod in individual widgets, let's focus on this provider thing. In Riverpod terms, a provider ... umm ... *provides* a saved value to anyone that asks for it. To share values between otherwise encapsulated widgets, we'll write to a provider in one widget and then read from that same provider in another. But how?

With Riverpod, we no longer inherit from StatefulWidgets. Instead, we inherit from *Consumer*StateWidgets. Get it? You write a provider that *provides* a value and a consumer that *consumes* that value. Clever, no? This consumer has a ref property which can see the providers. Check it out ...

4. Inherit from ConsumerStateWidget

Every widget that needs access to shared data should be written slightly differently.

Don't do this:

```
class FavColor extends StatefulWidget {
  const FavColor({super.key});
  @override
```

```
  State<FavColor> createState() => _FavColorState();
}
class _FavColorState extends State<FavColor> {}
```

Instead, do this:

```
class FavColor extends ConsumerStatefulWidget {
  const FavColor({super.key});
  @override
  ConsumerState<FavColor> createState() => _FavColorState();
}
class _FavColorState extends ConsumerState<FavColor> {}
```

You see, the magic is that these Riverpod-supplied classes have a property called *ref*. And ref knows about all of the providers you created above. Now let's use it.

5. Read Data with ref.watch()

In a stateful widget, the best way to read data from a given provider is with ref.watch(theProvider), which will monitor the provider and trigger its widget to re-render when the value in the provider changes.

```
Color favColor = ref.watch(favColorStateProvider);
int favNumber = ref.watch(favNumberStateProvider);
Person favPerson = ref.watch(favPersonStateNotifierProvider);
```

Tip   You can read data with ref.read() also. It's just that ref.read() is bound one time only; ref.read() doesn't update live but ref. watch() does.

---

6. Write Data with ref.read()

Ironically, you can write with ref.read(). There are other ways, but this is the most straightforward. Just do this:

```
ref.read(favColorStateProvider.notifier).state = newColor;
```

When you assign the state of this provider, it will set the value and notify all the listeners – those who had subscribed earlier with ref.watch().

There you have it. You can setup, write to, and read from Riverpod providers. We'll stop there. There's a ton more to this robust and powerful package, but you've got the idea. We have limited pages to devote and Riverpod will undoubtedly change. So if you're ready to go deeper (and I recommend that you do), start here: `https://pub.dev/packages/riverpod`. It will steer you to Riverpod's home page and documentation for more.

Conclusion

The more stateful widgets we have, the more state needs to be passed around between them. This can get very complex very quickly so we look to packages like Redux, Hooks, raw_state, and ScopedModel, but most popularly, Riverpod to tame state. Sure, you could do it by hand using other tools and techniques like BLoC and InheritedWidget but that becomes unrealistic when your app approaches a large size.

Now that we can handle data *within* widgets and *among* widgets, let's see how to handle data between our app and a server somewhere. Let's look at making HTTP calls to read data and write data. Read on!

CHAPTER 9

Making RESTful API Calls with HTTP

We're getting really good at managing the state of our application, but where will that data come from? A local file? A local database? User-entered? Sure. Those are all possibilities, but real-world apps get real-world data from a server out in the cloud somewhere. Your application will make HTTP calls, hopefully asynchronous RESTful HTTP API calls. It'll wait for and process the response and usually display that data. Wow! That's a lot of buzzwords, am I right? In this chapter, we're going to learn what those things mean and how to handle HTTP requests and responses of all types in your Flutter app. Here's what we need to know:

- What is an API call anyway

- Making an HTTP GET or DELETE request

- Making an HTTP POST, PUT, or PATCH request

- Handling the response in the simplest way

- Cleaner handling with FutureBuilder and StreamBuilder

- Even cleaner handling with strongly typed objects

© Rap Payne 2024
R. Payne, *Flutter App Development*, https://doi.org/10.1007/979-8-8688-0485-4_9

That'll be our plan for this chapter. That, and getting in some hands-on practice with an API service that allows HTTP requests. And to make sure everyone is on the same page (pun definitely intended), we should probably start with what exactly an API is. Feel free to skim it or skip altogether if you're already familiar.

What Is an *API* Call?

Flutter apps already have the capability to read from a tiny, localized database. But it cannot read from one that is located *elsewhere*. In other words, you can't just connect to a SQL Server/MongoDB/PostgresSQL database and read or write records. Can't be done, not even if you have database credentials. I mean, think about the security implications if public apps could connect from anywhere and directly modify data. So what developers do instead is create a server-side program to read and write in a controlled way and then expose that program on your network or the Internet at a particular address with a particular protocol, usually https.

To read this server-side data, any user can make http requests after having sent their credentials in the form of username/password or better yet, a unique and secret key called an API key.

There's that term *API* again. It stands for Application Programming Interface. It means different things in different situations, but its default meaning has come to be any Internet address to which developers can send http requests for the purpose of reading and writing data. There are tons of publicly available APIs and many options for creating your own.

When an API responds, it returns with a stream of data that is almost always in JSON[1] format.

---

[1] Read up on JSON here: https://json.org

The Flavors of API Requests

Communication with API servers is done in one of just a few flavors
(Table 9-1).

Table 9-1. *HTTP methods and descriptions*

HTTP method	Intent	Notes
GET	Reading records	Like a database read, merely asking for data from a server
DELETE	Deleting records	Delete the record pointed to by the supplied ID. No data is returned
POST	Inserting new records	Create a new record even if there's already a record like this one
PUT	Replacing existing records	Clobber the existing record with this one. Delete the old record completely and add this one in its place
PATCH	Updating existing records	Keep the old record in place but update its fields with the data from this request

There's also HEAD, CONNECT, OPTIONS, and TRACE for other types
of requests. These are seldom used by typical apps. Read about them at
`http://bit.ly/HTTPMethods` if you want.

It is rare for developers to use anything other than GET, POST, PUT,
PATCH, and DELETE. They're all done in Flutter by using one Dart library
which you'll get by importing http.dart.

First, you'll add the http package to the dependencies section of your
pubspec.yaml. When you add and run "flutter pub get," the package will be
downloaded from `https://pub.dev/packages/http`.

Then you'll import http.dart in any Dart file that needs to make these requests:

```
import 'package:http/http.dart';
```

This will expose the http class which has methods corresponding to each HTTP method. Now, let's look at sending requests using this library.

Making an HTTP GET or DELETE Request

We'll begin with GET and DELETE requests first because they are the simplest; they never have a body.[2] In fact, the only complexity is that HTTP requests are done asynchronously. They return a Future[3] which you either need to handle with a .then() or await it. So maybe make your request like this:

```
Uri uri = Uri.parse('https://us.com/people/1234');
Response response = await get(uri);
print(response.statusCode); // 200, we hope 🤞
Map<String, dynamic> person = json.decode(response.body);
print(person['name']);
print(person['phone']);
print(person['email']);
```

---

[2] This is a hotly debated topic. While the HTTP spec is silent, RFC 2616 hints that a body is ignored in a DELETE request but doesn't explicitly forbid it. Some servers will ignore the body. Other servers will ignore the entire request. While others throw a 400 error. Either test it on your server or play it safe and omit the body.

[3] If you want to understand Futures a bit better, take a read through Appendix B, "Futures, Async, and Await."

or with a .then() like this:

```
get(uri).then((Response res) {
  print(res.statusCode); // 200, we hope 🤞
  Map<String, dynamic> person = jsonDecode(res.body);
  print(person['name']);
  print(person['phone']);
  print(person['email']);
});
```

Delete requests are done in the same way. In fact, they are often simpler because they often have no response values. The DELETE either succeeds and has no return value or fails with a 400- or 500-series response:

```
Response response = await delete(uri);
```

Caution   When making HTTP requests of any type, you should always encode the URL before sending. This will help to ensure that the URL is valid and can also help with security, especially when taking input from the user. You can do this with Uri. encodeComponent(), Uri.encodeQueryComponent(), and/or with Uri. encodeFull(). Call Uri.encodeFull like this:

```
String url = Uri.encodeFull('http://us.com/api/
ppl?query=Jo Ki');
```

For simplicity's sake, we're going to omit encoding in the examples. But in the real world, remember to do this.

Making an HTTP PUT, POST, or PATCH Request

PUT, POST, and PATCH are very similar to GET and DELETE. The biggest difference is that PUT, POST, and PATCH all require a body for the request – usually a string with JSON-formatted keys and values:

```
String payload = '''
  {"first": "Kamala", "last": "Khan", "id": 374}
''';
Response response = await post(uri, body: payload);
```

This response is unwrapped just as with GET and DELETE requests.

Note   With POST, PUT, and PATCH, we're sending data from the client to the server. It is prudent and sometimes required to also tell the server how we've encoded that data. We'll do that in an HTTP header that we include in the request. Provide a key called "Content-Type" with a value of "application/json". And we'll do that like so:

```
Map<String, String> headers= {'Content-Type':
'application/json'};

Response res = await post(url, headers:headers,
body:payload);
```

While we're on the subject, there are many header variables that you might find helpful like Accept, Accept-Encoding, Authorization, Content-MD5, Cookie, Date, Host, If-Modified-Since, and others. Read about them here: https://en.wikipedia.org/wiki/List_of_ HTTP_header_fields#Request_fields.

Making HTTP requests from an API wasn't so bad, now was it? Very quickly we've made our Flutter apps capable of making requests, deserializing the response, and printing that to the debug console. But Flutter is all about displaying that data in cool-looking widgets. So how do we integrate the requests into widgets?

HTTP Responses to Widgets

There's a handful of ways to wait on the Future to resolve and then display it. We're going to simplify things by showing you three:

1. The brute force way

2. FutureBuilder

3. StreamBuilder

Brute force is obvious and easy to understand, but I think you'll like FutureBuilder/StreamBuilder because they are cleaner and more elegant.

Brute Force – The Easy Way

You already have all the tools you need to display the data: you understand Futures and you know how to tell the stateful widget to redraw itself with new data – setState(). So it can be as simple as putting a setState() inside the .then() or after the await:

```
Uri uri = Uri.parse('http://us.com/api/people/12345');
Response response = await get(uri);
Map<String, dynamic> body = json.decode(response.body);
String first = body['name'];
String email = body['email'];
String imageUrl = body['profilePictureUrl'];
Widget card = Stack(
```

```
    children: <Widget>[
      Image.network(imageUrl,
        height: 300, width: 300, fit: BoxFit.cover),
      Text("$name"),
    ],
  );
  setState(() =>_cardWidget = card);
```

And of course as long as your build method is displaying *card* somewhere, it will be rendered with proper data as soon as the Future is resolved which only happens once the HTTP GET request returns data. Piece of cake! But it isn't the most elegant thing.

FutureBuilder – The Clean Way

A better solution may be the FutureBuilder widget. If you're ever in a spot where you have a Future that, when fulfilled, has data that must be rendered in a Flutter widget, look to FutureBuilder. Does this scenario sound familiar? It should because it is the major reason we have Futures in Flutter. The simple code example from earlier can be done much more cleanly with a FutureBuilder:

```
FutureBuilder(
  future: get(uri),
  builder: (ctx, AsyncSnapshot<dynamic> snapshot) {
    if (snapshot.connectionState != ConnectionState.done) {
      return const CircularProgressIndicator();
    }
    if (snapshot.hasError) {
      return Text('Oh no! Error! ${snapshot.error}');
    }
    if (!snapshot.hasData) {
```

```
        return const Text('Nothing to show');
      }
      final Map<String, dynamic> body =
          json.decode(snapshot.data.body);
      final int statusCode = snapshot.data.statusCode;
      if (statusCode > 299) {
        return Text('Server error: $statusCode');
      }
      String first = body['name'];
      String imageUrl = body['profilePictureUrl'];
      return Stack(
        children: <Widget>[
          Image.network(imageUrl,
            height: 300, width: 300, fit: BoxFit.cover),
          Text("$name"),
        ],
      );
    },
  );
```

There's no need for a setState() since the FutureBuilder has access to the Future itself so it knows when and how to redraw itself. In the preceding example, you can see how it is capable of rendering something different for each situation: a ProgressIndicator while we're waiting on the resolution of the Future, an error if something is wrong, a notification if the Future has nothing in it, and of course the widget when the data arrives successfully!

> **Caution**   Always check snapshot.hasData and/or snapshot.hasError before accessing snapshot.data. Also be careful about the HTTP status code which can be found in response.statusCode. If that number is in the 400s or 500s, you've gotten a valid response from the server, but it is a problem and your data will be null.

StreamBuilder

What FutureBuilder does with futures, StreamBuilder does with streams. These two classes are nearly identical, having the same format, using the same shape of snapshots, and checking snapshot.hasErrors and snapshot. hasData. But sometimes we're not dealing with a single return of data as with a future, we're dealing with a *stream* of data that may hit us in spurts or waves. When this is the situation, you'll want to use a StreamBuilder instead:

```
StreamBuilder(
  stream: anythingThatReturnsAStream(),
  builder: (BuildContext ctx, AsyncSnapshot<dynamic> snapshot){
    // Everything below this is pretty much the
    // same as FutureBuilder but the data is a
    // collection of documents, each being a record
    if (snapshot.connectionState != ConnectionState.done) {
      return const CircularProgressIndicator();
    }
    if (snapshot.hasError) {
      return Text('Oh no! Error! ${snapshot.error}');
    }
    if (!snapshot.hasData) {
      return const Text('Nothing yet. Please wait ...');
    }
```

```
return ListView.builder(
  itemCount: snapshot.data.documents.length,
  itemBuilder: (BuildContext context, int i) {
    String first = snapshot.data.documents[i]['name'];
    String imageUrl =
              snapshot.data.documents[i]['imageUrl'];
    return Stack(
      children: <Widget>[
        Image.network(imageUrl,
          height: 300, width: 300, fit: BoxFit.cover),
        Text("$name"),
      ],
    ),
  },
);
);
},
);
```

Tip   Writing code like this, code that wakes up and updates itself based on newly arriving data has a term: *reactive programming*. Reactive programming happens when we make our app aware of its external influences and tell it to react somehow. You may have heard of reactive extensions like rxJava, rxJS, and rx.NET which are libraries with classes and functions made for this style. Well, there is one for Flutter unsurprisingly called rxDart. You can find it at https://github.com/ReactiveX/rxdart.

Strongly Typed Classes

At this point, you now know how to make HTTP calls against an API, and when you get a response, you know how to unwrap that data and use it. This puts us in a great position to convert that data into a strongly typed class using the typed deserialization pattern.

Note   This is not required in order to make HTTP calls. It is merely a cleaner way of processing the call and pulling it into a structure that is predictable. HTTP data is by nature unstructured. This is a best practice used by many Flutter developers but is by no means required. So if you don't like it, feel free to skip it.

Typed deserialization happens in three simple steps:

1. Create the business class.

2. Write a .fromJSON() method and/or a .fromJSONArray() method.

3. When reading from HTTP calls, use .fromJSON() to hydrate the object.

Create a Business Class

Let's say we're reading and writing data for people. We should create a Person class:

```
class Person {
  String? name;
  String? email;
  String? imageUrl;
}
```

Write a .fromJSON( ) Method

This should be a static method that will return an instance of the business class, Person in this case:

```
class Person {
  // More class code here
  static Person fromJson(String jsonString) {
    Map<String, dynamic> data = jsonDecode(jsonString);
    return Person()
      ..name = data['name']
      ..email = data['email']
      ..imageUrl = data['imageUrl'];
  }
  // and more class code here maybe
}
```

Note the use of Dart's cascade operators and omission of the *new* operator. Both are best practices also.

Use .fromJSON( ) to Hydrate the Object

The word *hydrate* literally means "add water." In this context, the data is the water, and we're creating a new Person object by adding the data to it. You read data from an HTTP service using the .get() method and you pass it into .fromJSON() like this:

```
// Make the HTTP call
final Response res = await get(url);
// Hydrate a Person from the response body - a JSON string
Person p = Person.fromJson(res.body);
```

See how clean and straightforward the code is?

I imagine that at this point, you'd like to exercise all of this newfound knowledge. Let's do that with a free API service next.

One Big Example

A real API service will involve a database with exposed GET, POST, DELETE, PUT, and/or PATCH endpoints which all require some hefty setup on the server. You're going to want to get there eventually, but unless you're a full-stack developer, that's for the backend people. For now, let's make use of JSONPlaceholder, a free service for testing APIs. Read about it at https://jsonplaceholder.typicode.com/guide.

Note   JSONPlaceholder accepts all types of RESTful requests, but for obvious reasons, they can't have the world PUTting, POSTing, and DELETEing data unauthenticated. So they don't actually change any server data. The code we write would change server data if they honored it, but since they don't, please don't expect to see your changes persisted.

If you want to test the server, point your favorite browser at https://jsonplaceholder.typicode.com/users, and you'll see the first ten people. Congratulations, you've just made a GET request. Do another one at https://jsonplaceholder.typicode.com/users/1, and you'll see the person with a user ID of 1. In fact, try a few different IDs to see different users.

The other three HTTP methods are less simple. You'll want to use a tool like cURL, Postman, or SoapUI that can make POST, PUT, or DELETE requests.

Method	URL	What happens
DELETE	`https://jsonplaceholder.typicode.com/users/1`	Delete person #1
PUT	`https://jsonplaceholder.typicode.com/users/1`	Update person #1
POST	`https://jsonplaceholder.typicode.com/users`	Create a new person

And how will we apply these in our app? Read on!

Overview of the App

On startup, the app will send a GET request to read a list of users and draw a screen to display them (Figure 9-1).

Figure 9-1. *A list of people cards*

When the user taps the trash can icon, the app will send a DELETE request to delete that person.

When they tap any user card, we'll show them a form with the user's current information (Figure 9-2) that they can then change and save. Hitting the save FAB will send a PUT request to the server.

Figure 9-2. *The "upsert" form to add or update a person*

Similarly, when they tap the "+" FAB on the people list, we'll show them this same form but with blank fields so they can create a new user.

Create the Flutter App

This project will be kind of fun because for the first time we're combining topics from throughout the book. First, create the flutter app with `flutter create people_maintenance`. Next, make sure the http package is installed.

```
flutter pub add http
```

Open main.dart and find your MaterialApp widget. Remove the "home" property and add two named routes to it:

```
routes: {
  '/': (_) => const ListPeople(),
  '/upsert': (_) => const UpsertPerson(),
},
```

Then make two new StatefulWidgets, one called "list_people.dart" and the other called "upsert_person.dart". We'll fill in their details in a minute. But first, it may be a good idea to create a business class to represent a Person object.

Making a Strongly Typed Business Class

Since we're working with Persons, it might be a good idea to create a Person class to hold each person. This very optional best practice may help us to avoid bugs serializing and deserializing the server data and give us a centralized place to manage all of our Person-related logic:

```
import 'dart:convert' show jsonDecode;
class Person {
  Person({this.id, this.name, this.email, this.phone});
  int? id;
  String? name;
  String? email;
  String? phone;

  // The typed deserialization pattern for a single person
  static Person fromJson(String jsonString) {
    Map<String, dynamic> json = jsonDecode(jsonString);
    return Person(
```

```
      id: json['id'],
      email: json['email'],
      name: json['name'],
      phone: json['phone']);
  }

  Map<String, dynamic> toJson() =>
    {'id': id, 'email': email, 'name': name, 'phone': phone};

  // The typed deserialization pattern for a List uses .map()
  static List<Person> fromJsonArray(String jsonString) {
    List<dynamic> json = jsonDecode(jsonString);
    return json
      .map((p) => Person(
          id: p['id'],   email: p['email'],
        name: p['name'], phone: p['phone']))
      .toList();
  }
}
```

list_people.dart

We'll soon read a list of people from the RESTful service and will want to display their data. The PeopleList widget is responsible for showing that list of people:

```
import 'package:flutter/material.dart';
import './people.dart';
import './person_widget.dart';
import './person.dart';

class ListPeople extends StatefulWidget {
  const ListPeople({super.key});
```

```
  @override
  State<ListPeople> createState() => _ListPeopleState();
}

class _ListPeopleState extends State<ListPeople> {
 @override
 Widget build(BuildContext context) {
   return Scaffold(
     appBar: AppBar(title: const Text('People')),
     body: scaffoldBody,
     floatingActionButton: FloatingActionButton(
       child: const Icon(Icons.add),
       onPressed: () {
         Navigator.pushNamed(context, '/upsert');
       },
     ),
   );
 }

 // Note how we pull out details to make the widget more
 // abstract for you. We do the same with PersonWidget below.
 Widget get scaffoldBody {
  return FutureBuilder<dynamic>(
    future: fetchPeople(), // How we'll get the people
    builder: (ctx, snapshot) {
      if (snapshot.hasError) {
        return Text('Oh no! Error! ${snapshot.error}');
      }
      if (!snapshot.hasData) {
        return const Text('No people found');
      }
      // Convert the JSON data to an array of Persons
```

```
  List<Person> people =
            Person.fromJsonArray(snapshot.data.body);
  // Convert the list of persons to a list of widgets
  List<Widget> personTiles = people
      .map<Widget>((Person person) => PersonWidget(
          person: person,
          editPerson: () => setState(() {
              Navigator.of(context)
                .pushNamed('/upsert', arguments: person);
            })))
      .toList();
  // Display all the person tiles in a scrollable ListView
  return ListView(
    children: personTiles,
  );
  },
 );
}
}
```

PersonWidget is the widget that draws each Person on the screen (Figure 9-3). We're sparing you the details as of right now since that's not the focus of this chapter. But you can look in the GitHub repository for the details.

Figure 9-3. *Each PersonWidget displays one person*

A GET Request in Flutter

Look back at getScaffoldBody() method. It has a FutureBuilder. The future property points to a method called fetchPeople() which simply makes a GET request to the URL that will respond with a JSON array of Person records:

```
const String _baseUrl =
                 'https://jsonplaceholder.typicode.com';

Future<Response> fetchPeople() {
  Uri uri = Uri.parse('$_baseUrl/users');
  return get(uri);
}
```

The GET request is pretty simple once you get the Flutter infrastructure created, huh?

A DELETE Request in Flutter

Each PersonWidget has a trashcan IconButton on the right. A tap on it calls deletePerson(), receiving the person we want to get rid of. This deletePerson() method should send an HTTP DELETE request, pointing to that person by ID:

```
Future<Response> deletePerson(person) {
  Uri uri = Uri.parse('$_baseUrl/users/${person.id}');
  return delete(uri);
}
```

upsert_person.dart

We've taken care of reading people and deleting a person. But adding a new person will require a form for the user to enter information. Sharp readers will notice that an identical form is needed for updating existing persons. To adhere to the DRY principle,[4] let's create one form and reuse it for both adding and updating.

```dart
class _UpsertPersonState extends State<UpsertPerson> {
late Person person;
 @override
 Widget build(BuildContext context){
  // Get the 'current' person set during navigation. If
  // this person is null, we're adding a new person and
  // we must instantiate one. If this person is not null,
  // then we're updating that person.
  Person? routePerson =
    ModalRoute.of(context)?.settings.arguments as Person?;
  person = (routePerson == null) ? Person() : routePerson;
  return Scaffold(
   appBar: AppBar(
    title: Text(
     (person.id == null) ? 'Add a person' : 'Update a person',
    ),
   ),
   body: _body,
   floatingActionButton: FloatingActionButton(
     onPressed: () {
       // Save the person
       upsertPerson(person);
```

---

[4] https://en.wikipedia.org/wiki/Don%27t_repeat_yourself

```
      // And go back to where we came from
      Navigator.pop(context);
    },
    child: const Icon(Icons.save),
  ),
  );
}

Widget get _body {
    // Look in github for the Form code.
  }
}
```

Notice that in the FAB's onPressed handler, we're saving the form data and calling upsertPerson(). Here's what that looks like:

A POST and PUT Request in Flutter

If it is an Add operation, we want to make a POST call. If it is an Update operation, we want to make a PUT call:

```
Future<Response> upsertPerson(Person person) {
  final String payload = '''
  {
    "id": ${person.id},
    "name":"${person.name}",
    "phone":"${person.phone}",
    "email":"${person.email}"
  }
  ''';
  final headers = {'Content-type': 'application/json'};
  // If id is null, we're adding. If not, we're updating.
  if (person.id == null) {
```

```
  Uri uri = Uri.parse('$_baseUrl/people');
  return post(uri, headers: headers, body: payload);
} else {
  Uri uri = Uri.parse('$_baseUrl/people/${person.id}');
  return put(uri, headers: headers, body: payload);
 }
}
```

Conclusion

Not too shabby, huh? We went from knowing almost nothing about reading and writing data via HTTP to a comprehensive example using some fairly advanced techniques like the typed deserialization pattern and the FutureBuilder widget.

If you followed my code examples above, your app reads HTTP data just great. But it still wouldn't look like the screenshots. You see, I used styles and theming to make it look pleasing to the eyes. Styling is still a bit of a mystery to us. Hey, let's unwrap that mystery in the next chapter!

CHAPTER 10

Styling with Themes

Styling your widgets isn't entirely new to you. We've touched on some minor styling features in prior chapters, and you've seen styling techniques in our code samples. But this is the chapter where we'll take a deep dive on styling. Finally!

You can always do low-level styling so we'll start with that. Then we'll progress to the more complex but cleaner way with themes. We'll bring the chapter to a close with the nitty-gritty of colors and custom fonts.

Thinking in Flutter Styles

Styling in Flutter borrows the best ideas from Android, iOS development, and web development. But it doesn't copy their techniques *exactly*. Flutter does things its own way, and it is a mistake to take the web analogies too far. Flutter's styling is not CSS. Whereas CSS has certain properties that are passed down to their children, Flutter styles are not inherited. You cannot set a font family on your custom widget, for example, and have all of the Texts and TextFields and buttons inside it suddenly begin rendering with that font. To make that kind of thing happen, we'll create and apply a theme. But first, let's learn how to apply styles to elements.

Individual Styles

We've peeked at this in prior chapters and in code examples. Most widgets will accept a style property and often style-adjacent properties like padding, borders, and so forth. You can and sometimes do manually set these values, usually when you have styling needs that only apply to one instance of one widget, like an individual Text widget.

Styling Text

```
Text(aString, style: TextStyle(
  fontSize: 12.0,
  fontWeight: FontWeight.bold,
  color: Colors.blue,
  fontStyle: FontStyle.italic,
)),
```

Text widgets have a *style* property which takes a TextStyle object (Figure 10-1).

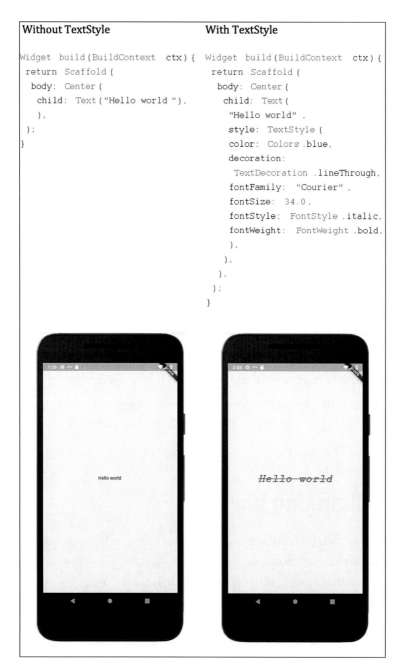

Figure 10-1. *With and without style*

You'll simply set the *style* property to an instance of a TextStyle widget and set properties. TextStyle supports about 20 properties. Here are the most useful:

- color – Any of the valid 16+ million colors

- decoration – TextDecoration.underline, overline, strikethrough, none

- fontSize – A double. The number of pixels tall to make the characters. Default size 14.0 pixels

- fontStyle – FontStyle.italic or normal

- fontWeight – FontWeight.w100-w900. Or bold (which is w700) or normal (which is w400)

- fontFamily – A string

fontFamily is a bigger topic which we'll deal with at the end of this chapter.

Many widgets have a style property, and if you need to set the style of just one widget, this is the best way. But best practice would be to avoid individual styles as much as you can. It's much better and cleaner to create and apply a theme.

Mass-Changing Values

True story. I had a near-finished app. It was a thing of beauty. I chose colors from my client's corporate logo, assuming they'd appreciate me conforming to their marketing scheme. Well, one of their colors was cordovan and I used it liberally. My client hated that color, thinking that its reddish hue was communicating "danger" or "error." And you know what? They were right! I just hadn't made that connection. So of course I wanted to change it throughout.

Now, imagine what I had to do. Go through the entire app? Find all of the occurrences of that color in the hundreds of Text widgets, borders, shadows, buttons, cards, and tiles? Nope. Because I used a theme, I changed it in one place while the client waited. In fact, we iterated with different colors until we found a color scheme that they loved. It was super easy, barely an inconvenience! Let's look at the right way to set styles with themes.

Themes

When you use a theme, you define the styles in one file at one time, up front. And why?

1. There's a consistent, cohesive look and feel across your entire app.

2. Style changes across the entire app become almost effortless.

To use a theme involves five fairly simple steps:

1. Set the ColorScheme

2. Set the TextTheme

3. Create widget-specific themes

4. Combine all these into the theme

5. Override the styles on lower-level widgets if needed

Let's work through these.

1. ColorScheme

The ColorScheme forms the basic colors of your app:

- primary – The main brand color

- secondary – An accent color

- tertiary – A less prominent color

- error – For spotlighting errors

- background – The general background color

- outline – For borders

- surface – For cards and container backgrounds

Four of these, primary, secondary, tertiary, and error, are each further broken into "on," "container," and "onContainer." For example, primary has

- primary – The main brand color

- onPrimary – A color that contrasts primary; good for readability

- primaryContainer – A good background color for primary

- onPrimaryContainer – Readable as text on a primaryContainer background

These are all colors that are scientifically selected to look beautiful together, and they're generated from a single primary color, the *seed* color.

```
var _scheme = ColorScheme.fromSeed(seedColor: <somecolor>);
```

Caution   ColorScheme.fromSwatch() is not deprecated per se, but it was designed to work with Material 1 and 2. If you're using Material 3 and up, use ColorScheme.fromSeed().

Take a look at the standard colors in three different schemes (Figures 10-2 through 10-4):

```
ColorScheme.fromSeed(
  seedColor:
    Colors.green)
```

Figure 10-2. *A green scheme*

```
ColorScheme.fromSeed(
  seedColor:
    Colors.blue,)
```

Figure 10-3. *A blue scheme*

```
ColorScheme.fromSeed(
 seedColor:
  Color.fromARGB(
   255, 191, 87, 0),)
```

Figure 10-4. *A burnt orange scheme*

You can of course create your ColorScheme object and set its every color manually but that would be a ton of work! Instead, let Flutter do the hard work of creating an initial scheme via ColorScheme.fromSeed() and supply your seed color.

Tip   In addition to the colors listed above, there's also shadow, scrim, surface, surfaceVariant, and more – about 30 in all. Don't worry about memorizing them. Now that you get the idea, you can look up the ones you want when the time comes.

If you decide to adjust one or more of the default colors, use copyWith():

```
ColorScheme _colorScheme = ColorScheme.fromSeed(
  seedColor: Colors.green,
).copyWith(
  error: Color.fromARGB(255, 191, 87, 0),
  onError: Colors.white,
);
```

This will set all the colors with one command.

2. TextTheme

Your textTheme is comprised of 15 TextStyles. Setting them will automatically set the styles for certain widgets. For instance, changing the bodyMedium textStyle will in turn change the appearance of every Text widget, every ListItem, and every Navigator that you add. Setting the labelLarge textStyle will in turn set every TextButton, every ElevatedButton, every FAB, and every Chip you add. You have these general groupings:

- Display

- Headline

- Title

- Body

- Label

And behind each of these, you have a small, a medium, and a large. Figure 10-5 shows how they look.

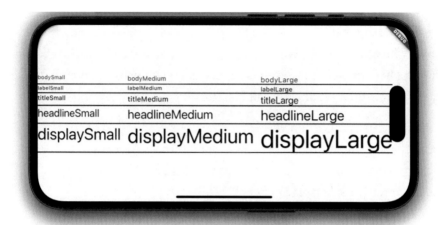

Figure 10-5. *The TextTheme text styles in actual size*

Again, I recommend using .copyWith() to change the defaults. Like if you wanted to make every Text widget larger, you may do this:

```
TextTheme _textTheme = const TextTheme().copyWith(
  bodyMedium: const TextStyle().copyWith(fontSize: 18.0),
);
```

Tip   .copyWith() is a familiar pattern in Dart. Many, many classes are written to have a .copyWith() method that allows you to make incremental changes to a copy of an instance. Look for this pattern and you'll be surprised how many times it turns up. In fact, write a .copyWith() method in your own classes and your fellow developers will thank you.

---

3. Widget-Specific Themes

Many of the other display widgets have styles that you can override when you don't like the defaults. For instance, what if you wanted to change the way that all AppBars look? And all ListTiles?

```
// Widget-specific themes
AppBarTheme _appBarTheme = const AppBarTheme().copyWith(
  foregroundColor: _colorScheme.onTertiaryContainer,
  color: _colorScheme.tertiary,
  titleTextStyle: _textTheme.displayLarge!
    .copyWith(fontFamily: 'Courier'));

ListTileThemeData _listTileThemeData = ListTileThemeData(
    tileColor: _colorScheme.secondary,
    textColor: _colorScheme.onSecondary,
    contentPadding: const EdgeInsets.all(10.0));
```

Note that these are much lower-level and only apply to those particular widgets. Many widgets carry their own themes consisting of styles that are particular to that widget type. And of course once set in the Theme and applied to the MaterialApp, all widgets of that type will adhere. You've actually got quite a few widget themes:

appBarTheme, textButtonTheme, elevatedButtonTheme, cardTheme, inputDecorationTheme, iconTheme, sliderTheme, tabBarTheme,drawerTheme, tooltipTheme, chipTheme, dialogTheme, pageTransitionTheme, floatingActionButtonTheme, NavigationRailTheme, snackBarTheme, bottomSheetTheme, popupMenuTheme, bannerTheme, buttonBarTheme, bottomNavigationBarTheme, timePickerTheme, outlinedButtonTheme, textSelectionTheme, dataTableTheme, checkboxTheme, radioButtonTheme, sliderTheme, switchTheme, progressIndicatorTheme.

4. Put Them Together in a Theme

It's time to put all of this together in a theme. We've written a lot of code already, right? Themes are more verbose than you'd anticipate, so I recommend creating it in a separate file, say in theme.dart:

```dart
ThemeData themeData = ThemeData(
  colorScheme: _colorScheme,
  textTheme: _textTheme,
  // Widget-specific themes only when needed
  appBarTheme: _appBarTheme,
  listTileTheme: _listTileThemeData,
  // Optionally set other specialized things here
  fontFamily: 'Courier',
  fontFamilyFallback: const ['monospace', 'serif'],
);
```

Then import that theme into your main.dart file and apply it to your MaterialApp:

```dart
import './theme.dart';
class MyApp extends StatelessWidget {
  @override
  Widget build(BuildContext context) {
    return MaterialApp(
      title: 'Themes and Styles Demo',
      theme: themeData,
      routes: {
        "/": (_) => const Dashboard(),
        ...,
      },
    );
  }
}
```

That's it! Run your app and observe the glory of your awesome design! Nothing else is needed. Unless, that is, you need to apply individual styles sporadically.

5. Override the Styles on Individual Widgets

Last step. Setting your ColorScheme, your TextTheme, and your individual widget themes establishes the default look and feel for your app. But sometimes we want the one widget to be specially styled. Maybe a Text() you have at the top of the page should function as a page heading. Or what if you want one button to look different. Like an "Are you sure?" button. Maybe we want that one – just that one – to stand out from the others. So occasionally we want to set the style on an individual widget. When you have a theme, the best practice is to create a style based on a theme style, using .copyWith() to extend it. Then apply it to your special widget.

```
// First, copy the default style & apply your customizations
TextStyle dangerButtonStyle = Theme.of(context)
  .TextTheme.labelLarge.copyWith(
  fontSize: 18.0,
  fontWeight: FontWeight.bold,
  color: Colors.red,
 );
```

```
// Use the custom style in your button widget
TextButton(
  onPressed: () => deleteEverything(),
  child: Text("Are you sure?", style: dangerButtonStyle),
);
```

Tip   We've seen that MaterialApp has a *theme*. It so happens that the theme is the lightTheme. MaterialApp also has a *darkTheme*. Create a darkTheme just like you did the regular (light) theme and point the MaterialApp to it. Now, your app can respond to the OS's light and dark theme changes.

Final Styling Thoughts

Before we leave the subject of styling, we really should briefly discuss colors and fonts. If these don't interest you immediately, feel free to skip to the end of the chapter. Come back to read this when you have a pressing need. But colors and fonts are not completely straightforward in Flutter. There are a few gotchas which we'll discuss.

A Word About Colors

Most Flutter styles are very narrowly applied; they only make sense for certain tightly defined situations. On the other hand, colors are applied nearly everywhere (Figure 10-6). Borders, text, backgrounds, icons, buttons, and shadows all have colors. And they're all specified in the same manner. For example, here's white Text in a red container with a yellow border, and all of those widgets are colored identically with the syntax "color: Colors.somethingOrOther":

```
child: Container(
  decoration: BoxDecoration(
    color: Colors.red,
    border: Border.all(color: Colors.yellow)
  ),
```

```
  child: Text('Colors!',
    style: TextStyle(color: Colors.white,),
  ),
),
```

Figure 10-6. *Colors are everywhere in Flutter*

And you see those colored blocks in the background? Those were created like this:

```
List<Widget> _randomColors() {
 Random rnd = Random();
 return List.generate(25,
   (int i) => Container(
    color: Color.fromRGBO(
     rnd.nextInt(255), rnd.nextInt(255),
```

```
    rnd.nextInt(255), 1.0),
  ));
}
```

So you can create any of the 16+ million colors with Color. fromRGBO(red, green, blue, opacity) where each of the three RGB colors is a number between 0 and 255 and the opacity is 1.0 for fully opaque and 0.0 for fully transparent. There's also a Color.fromARGB(alpha, red, green, blue) which does the same things except moves the opacity to the front as alpha which is a number between 0 (fully transparent) to 255 (fully opaque).

If you come from a web background, you might be more comfortable creating colors using hex numbers. This works also:

```
color: Color(0xFFFF7F00),
```

Caution   Be careful. That hex number is actually "ARGB" where the first two hexadecimal characters are the alpha channel. If you forget it, like Color(0xFFF700), you'll be painting it full transparent and you'll never see it. Just remember that if your colors don't show up, take that typical web hex number and put an "FF" in front of it.

Custom Fonts

There are some fonts that are built-in like Courier, Times New Roman, serif, and a bunch more. How many more? It depends on the type of device on which the app is running. Since we don't have control over the users' devices, the best practice is for you to stick to the default font family unless you install and use a custom font. Let's talk about how to do that.

Certain designers call for custom fonts when they design scenes. It turns out with Flutter, using custom fonts is easy to implement, and they work cross-platform. It involves three steps:

1. Download the custom font files which are in ttf, woff, or woff2 format. These are customarily stored in a root-level folder called fonts, but the name is up to you (Figure 10-7).

Figure 10-7. *Fonts are usually stored in a folder called fonts*

Tip   You can find some excellent and free fonts at `http://fonts.google.com`. Search through them by type, see samples, and download them easily.

---

2. Add the font files to the pubspec.yaml file under flutter/fonts so that the compiler is notified to bundle them in the installation file.

```
flutter:
  fonts:
    - family: MrDafoe
      fonts:
        - asset: fonts/MrDafoe-Regular.ttf
```

```
    - family: NanumBrushScript
      fonts:
        - asset: fonts/NanumBrushScript-Regular.ttf
```

3. Use the case-insensitive font name in the fontFamily
   property of the TextStyle widget like we talked about
   in the previous sections:

```
Text(loremIpsums[0]),  // Unstyled
Text(loremIpsums[1],   // Some, like Courier may be
                          built-in
    style: TextStyle(fontFamily: 'Courier'),),
Text(loremIpsums[2],
    style: TextStyle(fontFamily:
    'NanumBrushScript'),),
Text(loremIpsums[3],
    style: TextStyle(fontFamily: 'MrDafoe'),),
```

The preceding example might look like Figure 10-8.

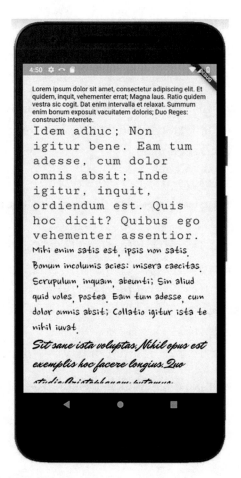

Figure 10-8. *Available fonts*

Conclusion

As you can see, the options for styling things in Flutter are near infinite.
Flutter styling is by no means the same as CSS. First, it is more verbose.
Second, it doesn't inherit. Some people may resent these characteristics,
but others will like the cleanness that it creates.

Regardless of how you feel about that, you've got to be impressed with the styling power that Flutter provides, especially when you think about how styles are organized in themes so we can present a consistent, professional look and feel throughout our app.

Now, for the moment you've all been waiting for … let's learn how to lay out our widgets in a scene!

CHAPTER 11

Laying Out Your Widgets

We've made a ton of progress, but a major topic remains – controlling the visual layout of your app's widgets. We need fine-grained control of how widgets appear on the screen – size, location, and spacing. Here's how we'll tackle this.

Our Approach

To master layouts, we must know how to do five things:

1. Layout the entire scene

2. Position widgets relative to each other

3. Fix overflows, like when your widgets don't fit on a screen

4. Handle extra space, like when your screen is bigger than it needs to be

5. Fine-tune the position

This will be our plan for the next five chapters, one step for each chapter.

© Rap Payne 2024
R. Payne, *Flutter App Development*, https://doi.org/10.1007/979-8-8688-0485-4_11

1. Layout the Entire Screen (a.k.a. Scene)

In the current chapter, we'll learn how Flutter thinks when it lays out. We'll set the look and feel of the entire app (with MaterialApp) and create the outer structure of the scene like the title and menus (with a Scaffold) (Figure 11-1).

Figure 11-1. *Title and menu appear at the top along with other things like action buttons*

2. Position Widgets Above and Below Each Other or Side by Side

When designing any scene, we break it into widgets and place them on the screen. For example, the following scene (Figure 11-2) must be broken into widgets. Since it is a list of people, we might create a bunch of custom PersonCard widgets (Figure 11-3), placing them above and below each other. We'd might do that with a Column widget.

Figure 11-2. *A Column can place widgets above and below each other*

Figure 11-3. *We might create a PersonCard widget*

Then in turn, each PersonCard widget should have an image side by side with text (Figure 11-4). How do you get the text next to the image? We'll use a Row widget. Also notice that the text is a series of data about that person. How do you get the text above and below? We'll use a Column widget again.

Figure 11-4. *Row widgets and Column widgets can be used to place things*

Placing widgets will be the subject of Chapter 12, "Layout – Positioning Widgets."

3. Handle Situations When We Run Out of Space and Overflow the Scene

In the scene with all of the PersonCards, we have more people than we have screen so we've overflowed it. This normally throws an error, but there are several ways to fix the situation. We'll look at the strategies in Chapter 13, "Layout – Fixing Overflows."

4. Handle Extra Space in the Scene

Hey, there's extra space on the right side of each Person. What if we wanted that space to be on the between the picture and text? Or what if we wanted to put some of that extra space on the left of the image? Chapter 14, "Layout – Filling Extra Space," will show us how to distribute that space in eye-pleasing ways.

5. Make Finer Adjustments in Positioning

And for the last step in layouts, you'll probably want to perfect your scene by making tweaks to padding, margin, and alignment. This will keep our scene from feeling crowded. What can we do to create a little elbow room? In Chapter 15, "Layout – Fine-Tuning Positioning," we'll learn to make the layout look a little more like Figure 11-5.

Figure 11-5. *Fine-tuned spacing*

Alright, so there's our plan for the entire section of the book. We'll do a deep dive into each of the five steps in a chapter each. Ready for step one? Let's go!

Laying Out the Whole Scene

Here's a tip for you: Apps should never surprise their users.[1] When apps do things in the way that the user expects, they think the app is friendly, simple, and easy. Users have been trained to see a status bar at the top followed by a title bar. And while other screen affordances will vary based on need, there are definite conventions. Flutter has widgets to make your layouts feel … well … *normal*.

---

[1] *Don't Make Me Think* by Steve Krug is a great read on commonsense usability.

MaterialApp Widget

The Root App widget creates the outer framework for your app. As important as it is, the user never sees the App widget because no parts of it are technically visible. It wraps your entire app, allowing an app title so that when iOS/Android moves the app into the background, it'll have a name. The App widget is where you'll apply the default theme for your app – fonts, sizes, colors, and so forth. It's also the place to specify routes.

You have three choices for an App, a MaterialApp, a CupertinoApp, or a custom App widget that you create.

Most Flutter widgets work in any of the three Apps. The App widget merely lets you choose your base look and feel. If you place Cupertino widgets in a CupertinoApp, they'll look exactly like iOS apps. If you place Material-conforming widgets in a MaterialApp, they'll look more like an Android app.

"Yeah, but I need it to look like iOS on iOS and Android on Android!", you say. Okay, I get it. That's doable. You can create your own custom App widget that inherits from WidgetApp and perform a lot of conditional drawing like this:

```
Platform.isIOS ? CupertinoButton(...) : ElevatedButton(...)
```

But, yikes! That's a lot of low-level code to write and frankly negates the benefit of cross-platform so most devs don't bother with this. In the community, over 95% of projects use MaterialApp. Only a small fraction use CupertinoApp or a custom App widget derived from WidgetApp. Using MaterialApp is standard practice.

	MaterialApp	**CupertinoApp**	**WidgetApp**
Conforms to standard	Google's Material Design Guidelines	Apple's Human Interface Guidelines	None
Look-and-feel	Google/Android	iOS	Generic and flexible
Real-world use	Most apps	iOS-first or iOS-only apps	Base class for custom App widget creation

Here's how a MaterialApp may look:

```
Widget build(BuildContext context) {
 return MaterialApp(
  home: MainWidget(),
  title: "My Cool App",
  theme: _themeDefinedElsewhere,
  routes: ({
   '/scene1': (ctx) => MyWidget1(),
   '/scene2': (ctx) => MyWidget2(),
   '/scene3': (ctx) => MyWidget3(),
  },
  debugShowCheckedModeBanner: false,
 );
}
```

The Scaffold Widget

Whereas the MaterialApp widget creates an **outer invisible** framework, the Scaffold widget creates the **inner visible** framework.

Scaffold has one purpose in life: to lay out the visible structure of each scene to give it the predictable and therefore usable layout that so many other apps have. It creates, among other things:

- An AppBar for the title

- A section for the body

- A navbar at the bottom or a navigation drawer to the left

- A floating action button

- A bottom sheet – A section that is usually collapsed but can be slid up to reveal context-aware information for the current scene

```
@override
Widget build(BuildContext context) {
 return Scaffold(
  appBar: MyAppBar(),
  drawer: MyNavigationDrawer(),
  body: TheRealContentOfThisPartOfTheApp(),
  floatingActionButton: FloatingActionButton(
   child: Icon(Icons.add),
   onPressed: () { /* Do things here */},
  ),
  bottomSheet: MyBottomSheet,
 );
}
```

All parts of the Scaffold are optional. That kind of makes sense because you don't always want a floatingActionButton or a drawer or a bottomNavigationBar. Our screen designs will dictate which parts we want and which we don't.

The AppBar Widget

To create a header bar at the top of the screen, use an AppBar widget
(Figure 11-6). This is strictly optional. But your users are totally going to
expect an AppBar for almost every app that isn't a game. You'll almost
always have a title. And you may want to add an Icon at the start. An Icon is
the *leading* property:

```
return Scaffold(
 appBar: AppBar(
   leading: Icon(Icons.traffic),
   title: Text("My Cool App"),
 ),
 /* More stuff here. FAB, body, drawer, etc. */
);
```

Figure 11-6. *The AppBar widget with a leading icon and a title*

One problem though. If you have the leading icon and also a
navigation drawer, then Flutter can't use that space to display the
hamburger menu (Figure 11-7):

```
return Scaffold(
 appBar: AppBar(
   /* No leading this time. */
   title: Text("My Cool App"),
 ),
 /* More stuff here. FAB, body, drawer, etc. */
);
```

Figure 11-7. *An AppBar without a leading icon is able to display a hamburger menu icon*

If you have a navigation drawer, you're probably going to want to omit the leading icon.

SafeArea Widget

Physical device screens are seldom neat rectangles. They have rounded corners and notches and status bars at the top. If we ignored those things, certain parts of our app would be cut off or hidden. Don't want that? Simply wrap the SafeArea widget around all of your body content, and it will constrain your app to rendering below notches, status bars, and rounded corners. Putting it inside the Scaffold but around the body is a terrific place:

```
Widget build(BuildContext context) {
 return Scaffold(
  drawer: LayoutDrawer(),
  body: SafeArea(
   child: MyNormalBody(),
  ),
  floatingActionButton: FloatingActionButton(
   child: Icon(Icons.next),
   onPressed: () {},
  ),
 );
}
```

Flutter's Layout Algorithm

Brace yourself, friends. This final section of the chapter is not for the faint of heart. It's some pretty high-level thinking but to just skip it would be a disservice to you. Once you get your head around how Flutter lays out, so many widgets and their proper usage suddenly make sense. Without this understanding, we just hack at the code until it works – barely. This is frustrating and produces easily-breakable code.

So dig deep with me and let's talk about Flutter's layout algorithm. We'll start with …

The Dreaded "Unbounded Height" Error

I guarantee that at some point in your career, you're going to see Flutter throw this error:

```
═══╡ Exception caught by rendering library ╞═══════════════
The following assertion was thrown during performResize():
Vertical viewport was given unbounded height.
Viewports expand in the scrolling direction to fill their
container. In this case, a vertical viewport was given an
unlimited amount of vertical space in which to expand. This
situation typically happens when a scrollable widget is
nested inside another scrollable widget. If this widget is
always nested in a scrollable widget there is no need to use
a viewport because there will always be enough vertical space
for the children. In this case, consider using a Column or
Wrap instead. Otherwise, consider using a CustomScrollView to
concatenate arbitrary slivers into a single scrollable.
```

It's not the most developer-friendly error message, is it? Most of us would have no hope of understanding the problem in our code with that error message. Similar messages may say "RenderFlex children have non-zero flex" error. Or "RenderViewport does not support returning intrinsic dimensions." None of these are very helpful. If they were being kind, they'd have said something like:

══╡ You're doing it wrong ╞══════════════════════

The ListView you're drawing wants to be infinitely tall and it needs a parent widget that will keep it reasonably short. Maybe tell it to be small by wrapping it with an Expanded widget?

Now wouldn't that have been clearer? You'd understand the problem and how to fix it.

Let me help you interpret what Flutter is trying to tell us; certain widgets want to fill all the available space. In other words, they're greedy. They need a parent to constrain them. If they're inside of a parent who refuses to provide that constraint, Flutter freaks out because it can't draw something infinitely tall. Here's some code to illustrate the problem.

This code draws a header and 20 random Text()s in a Column(). It looks just fine (Figure 11-8):

```
Widget build(BuildContext context) {
 List<Text> randomTexts = List.generate(20,
  (i) => Text("Random number: ${Random().nextInt(1000)}-$i"));
 return Column(
    children: [
      Text("Some random strings for you", style: big),
      Column(
        children: randomTexts,
      ),
    ],
 );
}
```

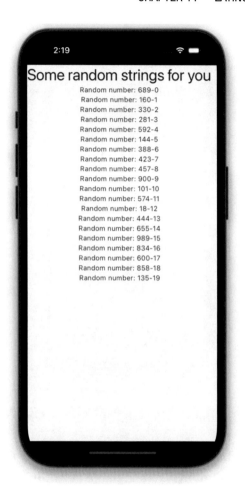

Figure 11-8. *A short Column draws just fine.*

Increase that number to 80 random Text()s and we overflow the viewport (Figure 11-9).

Figure 11-9. *A Column with too many children overflows the screen*

That's ugly, but that's not a runtime error. What should we do? I know! Let's make the list of randomTexts scrollable by putting them in a ListView. This is a perfectly logical thought.

```
@override
Widget build(BuildContext context) {
 List<Text> randomTexts = List.generate(80,
  (i) => Text("Random number: ${Random().nextInt(1000)}-$i"));
 return Column(
```

```
  crossAxisAlignment: CrossAxisAlignment.center,
  children: [
    Text("Some random strings for you", style: big),
    ListView(
      children: randomTexts,
    ),
  ],
);
}
```

All we did was change one widget from Column to ListView and BOOM! It blows up. See? The Column() doesn't think it's her responsibility to limit any children's height. "Be as big as you'd like," Column says. ListView will try to be as big as her parent will let her. Since ListView's parent isn't limiting her, she will be infinitely tall.

To be blunt, this is a symptom of the developer not really understanding how Flutter handles layouts. So let me try to explain Flutter's layout algorithm in hopes of predicting and therefore avoiding snafus like the preceding example. Then I'll explain a way to solve it.

The Algorithm Itself

Your widgets will always have a root widget at the top of your main method. It has branches and branches of branches and on and on. Let's call this the render tree (Figure 11-10). Flutter has to decide how big to make each widget in the tree. It does so by asking each widget how big it would prefer to be and asking its parent if that is okay.

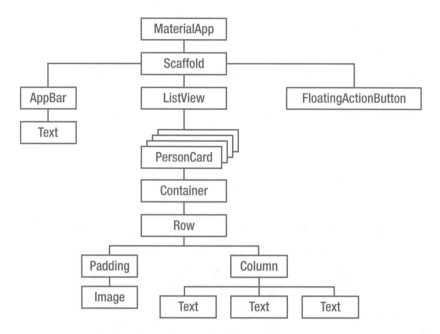

Figure 11-10. *Every scene has a widget tree*

Flutter travels down the tree starting at the top. It reads the BoxConstraints (max width and max height) of the root widget. It remembers them and then talks to each child. For each child, it communicates its BoxConstraints to them and then travels to the grandchildren. It keeps doing this all the way to the end of every branch. We call this the leaf level.

It then asks each leaf its RenderBox – how big it would prefer to be. Some children are greedy and say "as big as possible." Others take up a smaller amount. Flutter allows the leaf to be drawn at its preferred size *within the constraints* of all of its ancestors. If the preferred size is too big for its parent's BoxConstraints, Flutter clips it at runtime – something we work very hard to avoid! If the preferred size is too small, Flutter pads it with extra space until it fits.

It then goes back up a level and tries to fit those branches inside their common parent which has its own constraints. And so on all the way back up to the top.

The result is that each child gets to be its favorite height and width – as long as its parent allows it. And no parent has a final size until all of its child do.

So you can see how we'd get the "unbounded height" error. If we had a child who tries to be as large as it can and it doesn't have a parent to tell it to stop, Flutter panics because the child is now infinitely tall.

To solve the problem, the parent simply needs to instruct its child to stop growing. In our ListView/Column example, there are several solutions. One is to swap the Column and the ListView. A column isn't greedy so it can live in a ListView. But then the header Text scrolls off the page. Another is to wrap the ListView in a SizedBox which locks in the size exactly or a LimitedBox which provides a maxWidth and maxHeight. But those solutions are both clumsy. A third method is to wrap the ListView in an Expanded. We'll cover Expanded in detail in a few chapters but works in our favor in this case because the Expanded expands to take up the remaining (not infinite) space and tells its child that it now has BoxConstraints. Perfect! Here is all we need to do:

```
Widget build(BuildContext context) {
 List<Text> randomTexts = List.generate(80,
  (i) => Text("Random number: ${Random().nextInt(1000)}-$i"));
 return Column(
    crossAxisAlignment: CrossAxisAlignment.center,
    children: [
      Text("Some random strings for you", style: big),
      Expanded(         // <-- Add this widget
        child: ListView(
          children: randomTexts,
        ),
```

```
      ),
    ],
  );
}
```

Conclusion

Do you see why I said it's important to understand the layout strategy? Until you get your head around it, you're just guessing the solution. It's a lot of work to understand them all, but it's worth the effort.

Flutter has a ton of widgets to control size and position. For the next few chapters, we're going to study the most critical of those layout widgets – the ones you absolutely must know. We'll start with Row and Column.

CHAPTER 12

Layout – Positioning Widgets

Remember that the steps to the visual portion of an app are

1. Layout the entire scene

2. Position widgets relative to each other

3. Fix overflows, like when your widgets don't fit on a screen

4. Handle extra space, like when your screen is bigger than it needs to be

5. Fine-tune the position

In the last chapter, we studied Flutter's layout algorithm and we've learned how to set ourselves up for layouts with MaterialApp, Scaffold, and it's typical children. It's time to move on to step two, Rows and Columns.

Putting Widgets Next to or Below Others

Row and Column, as the names suggest, are made for laying out widgets side by side (Row, Figure 12-1) or above and below (Column, Figure 12-2). Other than how they lay out their children, they're nearly identical.

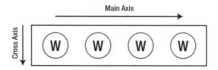

Figure 12-1. *A Row widget lays out side by side*

```
Row(
 children: <Widget>[
  SomeWidget(),
  SomeWidget(),
  SomeWidget(),
 ],
),
```

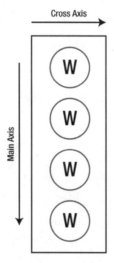

Figure 12-2. *A Column widget lays out above and below*

```
Column(
 children: <Widget>[
  SomeWidget(),
  SomeWidget(),
```

```
  SomeWidget(),
 ],
),
```

Notice that they both have a children property which is an array of widgets. All widgets in the children array will be displayed in the order you add them. You can even have rows inside columns and vice versa as many levels deep as you like. In this way, you can create nearly any layout imaginable in any app.

Rows and Columns will be your go-to layout widgets. Yes, there are others, but these two are your first calls.

Responsive Design

Responsive design originated in the early 2010s as the Web transitioned from desktop-dominated browsing to a world of smartphones and tablets, requiring websites to adapt to the new landscape of diverse screen sizes. A web app adjusts its layout in response to the screen size and orientation of the device on which it's being viewed. See what I did there? It's a *design* that is *responsive* to the screen size and orientation.

Responsive Design in Flutter

Flutter UIs need to adapt to mobile devices. Responsive Design ensures that your app's layout adjusts to different screen sizes and orientations, whether a user is holding their phone in portrait mode or has rotated it to landscape.

Imagine using your app in portrait mode. The layout is clean and all the elements are easy to tap and read. However, when rotated to landscape, the device text might overflow, buttons become too close together, or elements are hidden entirely. Using the Flex widget with

MediaQuery enables you to create a UI that intelligently adapts to the available space. This ensures a frustration-free experience for users, regardless of how they choose to hold their device.

Flex and MediaQuery

Just like a Row or Column, the Flex widget puts its children side by side or above and below. But Flex is flexible. It has an orientation property, vertical or horizontal.

- A Flex with orientation horizontal is exactly a Row().

- A Flex with orientation vertical is exactly a Column().

Note that this orientation property can be made conditional. That's where MediaQuery comes in.

MediaQuery gets certain data from the device itself.

- MediaQuery.sizeOf(context) – Width and height

- MediaQuery.displayFeaturesOf(context) – Camera holes, notches, etc.

- MediaQuery.platformBrightnessOf(context) – Light or dark mode

- MediaQuery.textScaleFactorOr(context) – Current font sizing

- MediaQuery.viewInsetsOf(context) – How much padding is the device applying?

- MediaQuery.devicePixelRatioOf(context) – Pixel density

> **Note**   As far as Flutter is concerned, pixels are actually *logical* pixels. You iOS developers call them *points*, and Android devs call them *density-independent pixels*. MediaQuery. devicePixelRatioOf(context) helps us to determine the true pixel density should you ever need it.

- MediaQuery.orientationOf(context) – Landscape or portrait

This last one is the key. You're going to examine the orientation, and if it's landscape, we need a Row. Otherwise, it should be in a Column. Here's some code:

```
Flex(
 direction:
  MediaQuery.orientationOf(context) == Orientation.landscape ?
    Axis.horizontal : Axis.vertical,
 children: <Widget>[
  SomeWidget(),
  SomeWidget(),
  SomeWidget(),
 ],
),
```

Conclusion

You now have the ability to place widgets beside one another or above and below. You can even Flex them responsively when needed. But what happens if the layout engine just doesn't have enough screen real estate to show all the content needed? What do we do then? Let's look at that in the next chapter.

CHAPTER 13

Layout – Fixing Overflows

Your widgets will never fit your screen.

It would be an overwhelming coincidence if the elements fit perfectly in a scene. And if they ever fit perfectly, as soon as the app is run on a different screen size or rotated from portrait to landscape, that will change. So we need to handle two situations:

1. What if there's not enough space? (too many widgets in a given space)

2. What if there's extra space left over? (more screen than pixels taken up by the widgets)

These are both likely to happen *simultaneously* on different parts of your scene. Let's tackle insufficient space in this chapter and deal with too much space in the next.

Overflow Warning Bars

To overflow a container isn't a fatal error, but it's bad. When any widget overflows a screen at debug time, Flutter is kind enough to let you know by showing you an overflow warning (Figure 13-1). They're yellow-and-black stripes along with some tiny red text saying by how many pixels it has overflowed.

© Rap Payne 2024
R. Payne, *Flutter App Development*, https://doi.org/10.1007/979-8-8688-0485-4_13

Figure 13-1. *Overflow bars*

Tip   The warning appears only in debug mode. A production app will never show these overflow bars. Instead the widget will simply be clipped. I'm not certain that's better.

Our Options to Correct Overflows

In the real world, if you have a fixed size container, say a cardboard box, and need to put something in it that is too big to fit, what would you do?

1.   Fold or disassemble the contents (assuming they can be disassembled or folded).

2.   Squeeze the contents until they fit (assuming they're squeezable).

3.   Put it in multiple boxes.

Logically, those are our only options. Let's apply this same thinking to Flutter screens. We have the same three options:

1.   Allow the children to wrap (assuming they can wrap).

2.   Squeeze the children until they fit (assuming they're scalable).

3.   Allow the user to scroll.

Let's see how we do those three things in Flutter.

A Sample Problem to Solve

To illustrate our three options, we've been given a list of random lorem ipsum strings. I've created a custom widget called Word() that is merely a wrapper around a Text() with a style and some padding. I'll convert those strings into Word widgets with .map and put them in a Column like so:

```
Widget build(BuildContext context) {
  var wordWidgets = words.map((w) => Word(w)).toList();
  return Column(
    children: wordWidgets,
  );
}
```

Figure 13-2 shows what you might see from this code.

Figure 13-2. *Looks great in a Column*

203

So far so good? In a Column, it displays just fine – plenty of room. But when we make it a row:

```
Widget build(BuildContext context) {
  var wordWidgets = words.map((w) => Word(w)).toList();
  return Row(
    children: wordWidgets,
  );
}
```

We have an issue. All those words can't fit across this device and we get overflow bars on the right (Figure 13-3).

Figure 13-3. *Overflow bars show we've overflowed the screen to the right*

Remember, we have three options to solve the overflow. The first is probably the best in our scenario – allow the Word widgets to wrap in their row.

1. Allow the Children to Wrap

A Wrap widget will do as the name suggests. Its contents are allowed to wrap down as many lines as are needed to fit them all on the screen.

```
Widget build(BuildContext context) {
  var wordWidgets = words.map((w) => Word(w)).toList();
  return Wrap(
    children: wordWidgets,
  );
}
```

The only change we've made is change the word Row to Wrap. That's it. It'll now behave like in Figure 13-4.

Figure 13-4. *Wrapping the contents*

This is the ideal solution for any list of words like in our current situation. But most times, we're working with other types of widgets. Let's look at solution number two.

2. Squeeze the Children Until They Fit

If your widgets are compressible, a logical options is to squish them horizontally for Rows or vertically for Columns until they fit. Sound uncomfortable? It kind of is. And it doesn't often result in a predictable and pleasant presentation. But it's occasionally exactly what is needed.

One way we can make things smaller is to put them in a Flexible(). A Flexible() says to its kid "I'm going to make you smaller until you fit or until you're as compressed as possible. If you can't be squeezed enough, I'll just throw up my hands and quit." This means that Flexible is not a guaranteed solution.

Tip   Flexible only makes sense directly inside a Row() or Column().

A Flexible is wrapped around each child in the Row or Column:

```
Widget build(BuildContext context) {
  var wordWidgets = words.map((w) => Word(w)).toList();
  return Row(
    children: wordWidgets
              .map((w) => Flexible(child: w))
              .toList(),
  );
}
```

Note Iterable.map() merely takes an array of X and converts it to an array of Y. All we're doing in that code above is nesting *each* Word() widget in a Flexible() widget. Please don't be distracted by that. Your focus in this chapter should be on the Flexible and its impact on the scene – it makes each child work together to fit. (Still, you've got to admit that the .map() was a clean method of converting.)

Each Flexible, in communication with all the other Flexibles in the Row, squeezes its child along the horizontal axis producing the less-than-pretty outcome in Figure 13-5.

Figure 13-5. *Flexible widgets squeezing their children*

Another option for squeezing

Remember, Flutter has hundreds of widgets with much overlap in their purpose and functionality. If you want to squeeze the children and Flexible isn't doing it for you, look at FittedBox.

A child in a FittedBox will be shrunk and/or clipped according to the BoxFit you tell it. Remember BoxFit from Chapter 4, "Value Widgets"? All those values apply it to a FittedBox.

- fitWidth – Make the width fit exactly. Clip the height or add padding to top/bottom if needed.

- fitHeight – Make the height fit exactly. Clip the width or add padding to left/right if needed.

- cover – Fit the smallest dimension (width/height) that will fit. Clip the other.

- contain – Fit the biggest dimension (width/height) that will fit. Add padding to the other.

- etc., etc. Refer to Chapter 4, "Value Widgets," for more details.

Not the best option in this case but great when you know exactly how many things you want to squeeze and precisely how many pixels one or more can have.

3. Allow the User to Scroll

Our final option to fix an overflow is to allow the user to scroll. Frankly, this is the most often-chosen option, making perfect sense in most situations. It is the easiest option to understand and perhaps the easiest to implement. I saved the best for last!

As is typical of Flutter, there are many options for scrolling. We'll look at three, SingleChildScrollView, ListView, and GridView.

SingleChildScrollView Widget

A SingleChildScrollView is well named. It wraps a *single child* and allows you to *scroll*. Instead of clipping that child, Flutter will let the user swipe to scroll either horizontally or vertically (the default). Here's our code with a SingleChildScrollView:

```
Widget build(BuildContext context) {
  var wordWidgets = words.map((w) => Word(w)).toList();
  return SingleChildScrollView(
    scrollDirection: Axis.horizontal,
    child: Row(
      children: wordWidgets,
    ),
  );
}
```

And Figure 13-6 shows us how it looks. Hey, no overflow bars! Comparing to prior screenshots, you can see that the position of the text has moved.

Figure 13-6. *Wrapped with a SingleChildScrollView allows scrolling*

Tip   A SingleChildScrollView allows scrolling horizontally *or* vertically but not both. An InteractiveViewer widget allows both. If you need to show something too big in both dimensions, look into an InteractiveViewer which allows panning/scrolling in both directions and allows us to zoom in and zoom out by pinching. This is great for hi-res pictures or large maps.

The ListView Widget

A ListView does not have a child property, it has a *children* property. So if we converted our Row to a ListView and set its scrollDirection property to horizontal, it looks and behaves just like the SingleChildScrollView.

```
Widget build(BuildContext context) {
  var wordWidgets = words.map((w) => Word(w)).toList();
  return ListView(
    scrollDirection: Axis.horizontal,
    children: wordWidgets,
  );
}
```

But ListView has superpowers that SingleChildScrollView does not. ListView is much more memory efficient, and it is much more flexible.

ListView Is Memory Efficient

A SingleChildScrollView builds its child and all of its descendents in memory, no matter how big or how many, before it displays them. ListView is different. A ListView keeps track of which children are currently being displayed and which are just off-screen. It only builds those. Therefore, while the user is preoccupied reading or scrolling what is on screen, Flutter is busily building more widgets that may appear soon. If the user is scrolling down, Flutter will be building widgets below the current viewport. If the user is scrolling back up, Flutter builds the widgets above. Get it?

It also pages out of memory those widgets that have scrolled off, so no matter how big your list gets, only a few are ever in memory at a time.

You smart readers have already seen a couple of flaws in this. First, it is possible to scroll faster than Flutter can create widgets. That's no big deal; it'll just show empty spots for a moment and then displays widgets as soon as they're created. Second, if the user scrolls up and down and up and

211

down and keeps doing that, Flutter will have wasted some time disposing of and recreating the same widgets. Sure, these are issues, but they're minor, well worth the cost when you look at the efficiency you're gaining.

Tip   ListView is the best option when you have a massive – even infinite! – list of items to display. Only those near the viewport are in memory.

ListView Is Very Flexible

ListView has four different ways to use it:

1. New ListView – Normal use. It has a children property that takes a collection of static widgets.

2. ListView.builder – For dynamically creating children from a list of items.

3. ListView.separated – Like builder but also puts a widget *between* each item. Great for inserting ads in the list periodically. Read more at `http://bit.ly/ flutter_listview_separated`.

4. ListView.custom – For rolling your own advanced ListViews. Read more at `http://bit.ly/flutter_ listview_custom`.

Let's take a look at the first two options starting with the regular ListView.

Regular ListView

This version of ListView is great for a number of predefined, diverse widgets to display. All you do is set the children property to a list that you've defined already. Our code example above showed this.

But where ListView really gets fun is when you tell it to build a new widget from a list of things – people, products, stores – anything you'd retrieve from a database or RESTful service. For displaying an dynamic number of scrollable items, we'll want the ListView.builder constructor.

ListView.builder: When You're Building Widgets from a List of Objects

ListView's alternative constructor, ListView.builder, receives two parameters, an itemCount integer and an itemBuilder function. The itemBuilder function dynamically creates children widgets on demand. As the user scrolls, itemBuilder function runs, creating new items.

The itemCount property is an integer that tells us how many things we're going to draw so we usually set it to the length of the array/collection of things we're scrolling through. The itemBuilder function receives two parameters: the context and an integer which is 0 for the first item and increments each time it is run.

```
Widget build(BuildContext context) {
  return ListView.builder(
    scrollDirection: Axis.horizontal,
    itemCount: words.length,
    itemBuilder: (context, i) => Word("$i - ${words[i]}"),
  );
}
```

In this example, we're now adding an index to each printed word. Note how I've again scrolled to the right (Figure 13-7).

Figure 13-7. *ListView.builder dynamically builds each child widget*

Creating lists of widgets that scroll in rows or columns is great. But what if you had square widgets that needed to be scrolled?

GridView Widget

Let's adjust our example. Instead of being provided some lorem ipsum words, let's say you're given a list of people and we want to create a small, roughly square-shaped PersonCard widget for each with a photo and name. You probably want these to appear in rows and columns instead of a list. GridView has the same magic that a ListView has but draws things in a wrapping grid.

You'll set GridView's children property to the list of widgets you want to display just like you did with Row, Column, Wrap, and ListView. GridView will display them in a grid, populating across and then wrapping to the next row, resizing its space available until it just fits. And here's the greatest part, it automatically scrolls!

GridView has two constructors, GridView.extent() and GridView.count().

GridView.extent()

The word *extent* refers to the maximum width of the child. GridView will only let its kids grow to that size. If they try to get bigger, it puts another element on that row and shrinks all children equally until they just fit across the entire width. Take a look at this example:

```
Widget build(BuildContext context) {
  return GridView.extent(
    maxCrossAxisExtent: 300.0,
    children: _peopleList
        .map<Widget>((Person person) => PersonCard(person))
        .toList(),
  );
}
```

Notice in Figures 13-8 and 13-9 how the containers resize to something less than 300. GridView decides that it can fit two across in portrait orientation. But when rotated, those two would have resized to something bigger than 300 so it puts three on each row.

Figure 13-8. *GridView. extent() in portrait*

Figure 13-9. *The same GridView.extent() rotated to landscape mode*

GridView.count()

With the count() constructor, you specify how many columns you want *regardless of orientation*. GridView takes care of resizing its contents to fit. In the following example, we've told GridView.count() that we want four columns regardless of the orientation and the GridView sizes its children to fit exactly four across. They're pictured in Figures 13-10 and 13-11.

```
Widget build(BuildContext context) {
  return GridView.count(
    crossAxisCount: 4,
    children: _peopleList
```

```
      .map<Widget>((Person person) => PersonCard(person))
      .toList(),
  );
}
```

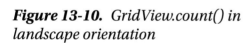

Figure 13-10. *GridView.count() in landscape orientation*

Figure 13-11. *The same GridView.count() in portrait orientation*

GridView.extent() is probably more useful because the contents stay approximately the same size regardless of the device, and that's a more typical desire than making the number of columns consistent.

Conclusion

It may be the most common situation to have more widgets than will fit on a device, and it may be the toughest problem to solve gracefully so it's a significant achievement to have made it through this far. In this chapter, we've given you a handful of solutions to that problem and some help in determining which solution is best for a given situation.

This was part three of our five steps to laying out a scene. Let's cover how to distribute extra space elegantly in part four, the next chapter.

CHAPTER 14

Layout – Filling Extra Space

We're deep into the process of laying out our scene. Remember, this is the process we're following.

1. Layout the entire scene

2. Position widgets relative to each other

3. Fix overflows, like when your widgets don't fit on a screen

4. Handle extra space, like when your screen is bigger than it needs to be

5. Fine-tune the position

We now know how to handle the entire scene, how to position widgets in relation to one another – above and below or side by side – and how to handle it when they're too big to fit. These are steps one, two, and three. Now let's take on the task of filling in the extra space in a Row or Column that may not look so good.

© Rap Payne 2024
R. Payne, *Flutter App Development*, https://doi.org/10.1007/979-8-8688-0485-4_14

What if There's Extra Space Left Over?

Compared to having too little space, this is a good problem to have. The only question you really need to answer is how to distribute the extra room. How much space do you want to allocate around each of the children widgets? You have several options. The easiest and quickest is to use mainAxisAlignment and crossAxisAlignment.

mainAxisAlignment

MainAxisAlignment is a property of the Row or Column (Figure 14-1). With it, you control how the extra space is allocated with respect to the widgets along the main axis – vertical for Columns and horizontal for Rows:

```
child: Column(
 mainAxisAlignment: MainAxisAlignment.spaceEvenly,
 children: [
  SubWidget(),
  SubWidget(),
 ],
),
```

You have a few choices.

start	end	center	spaceBetween	spaceEvenly	spaceAround
No space between them. All bunched up at the start. The default.	Same but at the end.	Same but we put space before the first and after the last	All remaining space is divided between each child widget	Same but some is saved for before the first and after the last	Same but the the spaces at the ends get half as much as the spaces between

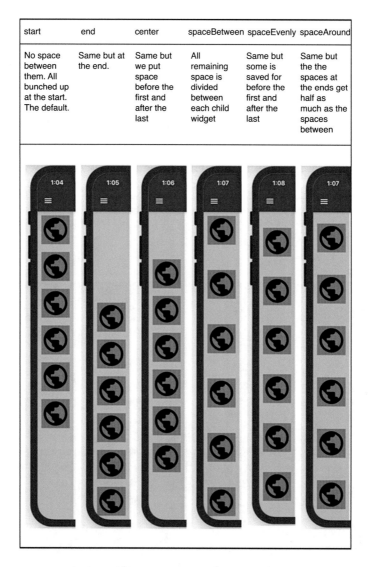

Figure 14-1. *mainAxisAlignment says how to distribute the extra space along the main axis*

crossAxisAlignment

crossAxisAlignment is also a property of the Row or Column; it determines where to put the extra space if the widgets are of different heights in a Row or widths in a Column. In Figure 14-2, we have one member that is purposely made wider than the others. Your options for crossAxisAlignment are shown in the figure.

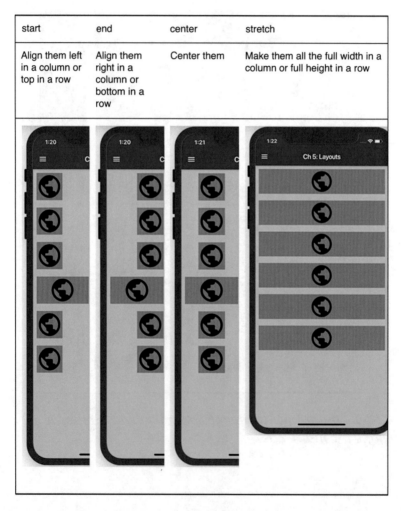

Figure 14-2. *crossAxisAlignment says how to distribute extra space along the cross axis*

There's also one more: baseline. But it only makes sense in a Row and when you're aligning Text()s of different heights. It lines up the base of the texts.

IntrinsicWidth

If you want the children of a Column to all be the same width but not necessarily the entire width of the screen, use the IntrinsicWidth widget. With crossAxisAlignment.stretch, they all stretch to the maximum width (Figure 14-3), but wrapped in an IntrinsicWidth, they'll all be the same size as the largest widget (Figures 14-4 and 14-5).

```
IntrinsicWidth(
 child: Column(
  mainAxisAlignment: MainAxisAlignment.center,
  crossAxisAlignment: CrossAxisAlignment.stretch,
  children: [ ... ],
 ),
),
```

Figure 14-3. *Without IntrinsicWidth, all children will stretch to the entire width*

Figure 14-4. *With IntrinsicWidth, they'll only be as wide as the widest member*

Figure 14-5. *With Intrinsic width and a wider member, all are made wider*

Notice the third child widget, how in Figure 14-4, it's long but grows in Figure 14-5. So you can see that as the width of the widest child increases, so do they all.

Expanded Widget

mainAxisAlignment is awesome if the spacing is cut and dried – you want equal spacing. This is the normal case. But what if you don't want spacing at all? What if you want the widgets to expand to fill the remaining space? Expanded widget to the rescue!

Let's take this code for an example. It's pictured in Figure 14-6.

```
Row(
  mainAxisAlignment: MainAxisAlignment.spaceAround,
  children: [
    SubWidget(),
    SubWidget(),
    SubWidget(),
    SubWidget(),
    SubWidget(),
    SubWidget(),
  ],
),
```

Figure 14-6. *This Row widget has lots of extra space*

When you wrap a Row/Column's child in an Expanded widget, it makes that child *flexible,* meaning that if there is extra space, it will stretch along the main axis to fill that space.

Here's the same thing but with an Expanded() around the second widget. See in Figure 14-7 how that widget now expands to gobble up all free space?

```
Row(
 mainAxisAlignment: MainAxisAlignment.spaceAround,
 children: [
  SubWidget(),
  Expanded(child: SubWidget()),
  SubWidget(),
  SubWidget(),
  SubWidget(),
  SubWidget(),
 ],
),
```

Figure 14-7. *The second widget is wrapped in an Expanded*

Note that the mainAxisAlignment now makes no difference because there is no extra space. It's all eaten up by the Expanded.

What if we add another Expanded? Let's put one around the third and fourth widgets also (Figure 14-8):

```
Row(
 children: [
  SubWidget(),
  Expanded(child: SubWidget()),
  Expanded(child: SubWidget()),
  Expanded(child: SubWidget()),
  SubWidget(),
  SubWidget(),
 ],
```

Figure 14-8. *Expandeds will divide the free space among them*

Note that the second one is now smaller because the extra space is shared with the third and fourth widgets, divided equally among them.

But wait! There's more! We can control how much space each Expanded gets. The Expanded has a property called the *flex* factor which is an integer. When the Row/Column is laid out, the rigid elements are sized first. Then, the flexible ones are expanded according to their flex factor (Figure 14-9). In the preceding examples, the Expandeds had the default flex factor of 1 so they got an equal amount of space. But if we gave them different flex factors, they'll expand at different rates:

```
Row(
 children: [
  SubWidget(),
  Expanded(flex: 1, child: SubWidget()),
```

```
Expanded(flex: 3, child: SubWidget()),
Expanded(flex: 2, child: SubWidget()),
SubWidget(),
SubWidget(),
],
),
```

Figure 14-9. *Expandeds have flex property to control how much extra space each gets*

Notice that the free space has still been allocated to the Expandeds but in the proportions of 1, 3, and 2 instead of evenly. So the one with a flex factor of 3 gets three times as much space as the one with a flex factor of 1.

Open Space with Expandeds

Maybe you want empty space between things like we had with mainAxisAlignment, but you also want to control how big those spaces are. This is where Spacer and SizedBox widgets can help.

Spacers put an empty space between widgets in a Row/Column. Each Spacer has a flex factor that plays well with all the other flex factors along this axis. So if you want to distribute space proportionally, Spacers will do the trick.

Tip   A Spacer is actually just an Expanded with an empty Container inside it.

227

But sometimes you want to have fixed empty space, like you know precisely how many pixels you want to leave open. This is where a SizedBox can help. SizedBoxes have height and width properties for fine-grained control. Figure 14-10 shows this.

```
Row(
 children: [
  SubWidget(),
  Spacer(),
  Expanded(flex: 1, child: SubWidget()),
  Spacer(flex: 2),
  Expanded(flex: 3, child: SubWidget()),
  Expanded(flex: 2, child: SubWidget()),
  SubWidget(),
  SizedBox(width: 10.0),
  SubWidget(),
 ],
),
```

Figure 14-10. *Spacer() and SizedBox() add free space back in but put you in control as to where and how much*

Conclusion

We've covered laying out the scene including what to do if there is extra space on the scene or there isn't enough of it. So let's learn the last of our five topics, how to fine-tune the spacing and position of widgets. We'll do this by exploring the box model.

CHAPTER 15

Layout – Fine-Tuning Positioning

We're almost finished with our learning journey, discovering how to lay out a Flutter scene. You've made it through all but the last step.

1. Layout the entire scene

2. Position widgets relative to each other

3. Fix overflows, like when your widgets don't fit on a screen

4. Handle extra space, like when your screen is bigger than it needs to be

5. Fine-tune the position

At this point, we can put anything in a scene and position them next to or on top of one another in any imaginable configuration. If we run out of space, we can handle the overflows. And if we have too much space, we can expertly distribute it.

Now if you're ready to play in the big leagues, let's talk about the fine-tuning. In this chapter, we'll learn fine-grained control over all the pixels on the screen and it will center around the box model.

© Rap Payne 2024
R. Payne, *Flutter App Development*, https://doi.org/10.1007/979-8-8688-0485-4_15

Container Widget and the Box Model

Flutter has borrowed heavily from other technologies including HTML and the Web which have the ideas of borders, padding, and margin. These are collectively called the box model. See Figure 15-1. They're used to create pleasant-to-the-eyes spacing around and between screen elements. It's a battle-proven concept that has worked great for the Web, so why not borrow it for Flutter?

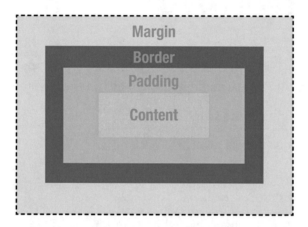

Figure 15-1. *The box model defines padding, border, and margin*

Let's say that we have a sized image that we want framed so to speak with a padding of 8, a margin of 10, and a border of 1. Flutter newcomers might try this first:

```
Image.network(
 _peopleList[i]['picture']['thumbnail'],
 padding: 8.0,
 margin: 10.0,
 border: 1.0,
),
```

This would not work because Image widgets don't have a padding, margin, or borders. But you know what does? Containers!

230

Web developers sometimes control the box model by wrapping elements in a generic container called a <div> and then applying styles to create pleasant spacing for our web pages.

Flutter doesn't have a <div>, but it does have a div-like widget called a Container which ... well ... *contains* other things. In fact, its entire life purpose is to apply layout and styles to the things inside of it. An HTML <div> can hold multiple things, but a Flutter Container only holds one child. It has properties called padding, margin, and decoration. We'll leave decoration for the end of this chapter, but padding and margin are awfully handy for creating nice-looking spacing:

```
Container(
 padding: EdgeInsets.all(8.0),
 margin: EdgeInsets.all(10.0),
 decoration: BoxDecoration(border: Border.all(width: 1.0)),
 child:  Image.network(thePicture),
),
```

EdgeInsets for Padding and Margin

Margin and padding might have been easier to learn if they had just allowed us to list four number values representing the four sides. (They couldn't make it easy, could they?) Instead, we use a helper widget called EdgeInsets.

- EdgeInsets.all(8.0) – Same value applied to all four sides evenly.

- EdgeInsets.symmetric(horizontal: 7.0, vertical: 5.0) – Top and bottom are the same. Left and right are the same.

- EdgeInsets.only(top: 20.0, bottom: 40.0, left: 10.0, right: 30.0) – Left, top, right, and bottom can all be different.

- EdgeInsets.fromLTRB(10.0, 20.0, 30.0, 40.0) – Same as the preceding one but less typing.

Also note that if you want padding only – no other formatting – the Padding widget is a shorthand.

```
Container(                        Padding(
 padding: EdgeInsets.all(5),       padding: EdgeInsets.all(5),
 child: Text("foo"),               child: Text("foo"),
),                                ),
```

These two are equivalent.

Alignment and Positioning Within a Container

When you place a small child widget in a large Container, there will be more space in the Container than is needed by its child widget. That child widget will be located in the top-left corner by default. You have the option of positioning it with the *alignment* property:

```
Container(
 width: 150, height: 150,
 alignment: Alignment(1.0, -1.0),
 child:  Image.network(
  _peopleList[i]['picture']['thumbnail'],
 ),
),
```

Those alignment numbers represent the horizontal alignment (–1.0 is far left, 0.0 is center, and 1.0 is far right) and the vertical alignment (–1.0 is top, 0.0 is center, and 1.0 is bottom). See Figure 15-2.

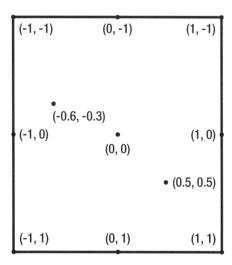

Figure 15-2. *Alignment coordinate system with 0,0 at the center*

But you will probably prefer to use English words rather than numbers when you can:

```
Container(
 width: 150, height: 150,
 alignment: Alignment.centerLeft,
 child:  Image.network(
  _peopleList[i]['picture']['thumbnail'],
 ),
),
```

Alignment can take on any of these values: topLeft, topCenter, topRight, centerLeft, center, centerRight, bottomLeft, bottomCenter, and bottomRight. Now, isn't that easier to write and easier for your fellow devs to read?

Tip   The Align widget is a shorthand for specifying the alignment and no other properties. The Center widget is merely a shorthand for centering.

These three are equivalent with the first being the most low-level and the last being the briefest and cleanest:

```
Container(
  alignment: Alignment.center,
  child: Text("foo"),
),
Align(
  alignment: Alignment.center,
  child: Text("foo"),
),

Center(
  child: Text("foo"),
),
```

Container Sizes Are Not Obvious

You may have noticed that I tried to slip width and height by you in that last section. Yes, you can tell a Container you want it to have a particular width and height, and it will comply *when it is able*. Width and height both take a simple number that can range from zero to double.infinity. The value double.infinity *hints* to be as large as its parent will allow.

Now, I know what you're thinking. "Rap, what do you mean by 'when it is able' and 'hints'? Aren't there any hard rules? I want Container sizes to be predictable!" And I completely agree. A Container's size is tough to predict until you know its rules. So, how does it decide then?

Remember two things. First, a Container is built to *contain* a child, but having a child is optional. Almost every time it will have a child. On the very rare occasions that a Container does not, we're using it to provide a background color or to create spacing for its neighbors/siblings. Second, remember that Flutter determines layout in two phases, down the render tree to determine Box Constraints and then back up to determine RenderBox (a.k.a. "size," remember?).

We go top down:

- Flutter limits max size by passing Box Constraints down into the Container from its parent.

- The Container is laid back as it tells its parent, "If my neighbors need some space, go ahead and take it. I'll be as small as you need me to."

- If height and/or width is set, it honors those up to its max size as determined by its Box Constraints. Note that it is not an error for you to list a size greater than its Box Constraints, it just won't grow any larger. This is why you can use double.infinity without error.

Tip   Setting height and width makes the Container super rigid; it locks in a size. While this is handy when you want to fine-tune your layout, the best practice is to avoid using them unless you have a darn good reason. You generally want to allow widgets to decide their own size.

Then we go bottom up:

- In the 1% of the time that it has no child, it consumes all the remaining space up to its max BoxConstraint.

- But most of the time, it has a child so the layout engine looks at the child's RenderBox.

- If the child's RenderBox is bigger than my BoxConstraints, it clips the child which is a big, fat problem. It's not technically an error, but it looks bad. So avoid it.

- If the child's RenderBox is within my BoxConstraints, there is leftover room. Flutter looks at the alignment property. If alignment is *not* set, we put it in the upper-left corner and make the container tight – it shrinks to fit the child.

- If alignment *is* set, it makes the Container greedy. This sort of makes sense when you think about it because how will it align top/bottom/left/right if it doesn't add space by growing?

- After all this, shrink as needed to honor the margins.

Yeah, it's complicated. This is why Container sizing is often misunderstood by Flutter devs. Play with it in a sandbox and you'll get accustomed to it. It takes a while.

Container Decorations

We promised at the top of this chapter to discuss borders. We did that because borders are not an obvious discussion. How do you add borders to Text? You can't. How about a background to an Icon? Nope. They don't have the capacity to have those decorations. But you know what does?

A Container. When you have styling problems like these, the answer is almost always to wrap widgets in a Container and put a decoration on the Container.

So understanding Container decorations solves a lot of problems for many, many widgets.

Containers have a catch-all styling property that is absent in most other widgets. It's called *decoration*. Here's an example of how to put a shadow on a container:

```
child: Container(
  width: 300.0,
  height: 300.0,
  decoration: BoxDecoration(
    color: Colors.purple,
    boxShadow: [
      BoxShadow(
        offset: Offset.fromDirection(0.25*pi, 10.0),
        blurRadius: 10.0,
      )
    ],
  ),
),
```

Figures 15-3 and 15-4 show boxes without and with shadows.

Figure 15-3. *Without a box shadow*

Figure 15-4. *With a box shadow*

And this is a terrific example of the wordiness with Flutter. In the Web, this would have been done in 17 characters. But in Flutter, we have to remember that boxShadow is an *array* of BoxShadows, each of which has an offset which takes a direction expressed in radians, a size expressed in pixels, and the blur radius is in pixels also. Sheesh!

Blur radius may call for additional explanation. The blur radius is the distance over which the shadow dissipates. It's like putting a lampshade on a lamp. Without a shade, the light is harsh and shadows are crisp. With a lampshade, the light is softer and the shadows are also. The larger the blur radius, the softer the shadow.

Caution   You cannot specify a color directly on a Container if you're also using a BoxDecoration. But don't panic; BoxDecoration also has a color property. Just move your Container's color property into the BoxDecoration for the same effect.

There are a number of other decorations available. Let's look at the most useful ones, border, borderRadius, and BoxShape.

Border

Just like you used a BoxDecoration for shadows, you also use them to put a border on a container. Here's a red border with four different widths (Figure 15-5):

```
Container(
 decoration: BoxDecoration(
  color: Colors.purple,
  border: Border(
   top: BorderSide(width: 10,color: Colors.red,),
   right: BorderSide(width: 20,color: Colors.red,),
   bottom: BorderSide(width: 30,color: Colors.red,),
   left: BorderSide(width: 40,color: Colors.red,),
  ),
 ),
)
```

Figure 15-5. *Borders with different widths*

While it's nice that Flutter allows us to have different widths and even different colored borders, how often will you use that? Usually all four sides will be uniform. So we commonly use the shorthand Border.all():

```
Container(
 decoration: BoxDecoration(
  color: Colors.purple,
  border: Border.all(width: 10, color: Colors.red,),
 ),
)
```

Much simpler. Yes, still verbose, but simpler.

BorderRadius

Rounded corners are a favorite look. You can make a Container rounded even if it doesn't have a border (Figure 15-6). You do this with BorderRadius:

```
Container(
 decoration: BoxDecoration(
  color: Colors.purple,
  borderRadius: BorderRadius.only(
   topLeft: Radius.circular(20.0),
   topRight: Radius.circular(60.0),
  ),
 ),
)
```

Figure 15-6. *BorderRadius on two corners*

We only gave it a topLeft and a topRight radius, but there is also a bottomLeft and bottomRight property. And although we appreciate the flexibility, it is not typical to use it. We ordinarily specify all four the same (Figure 15-7):

```
Container(
 decoration: BoxDecoration(
  color: Colors.purple,
  borderRadius: BorderRadius.all(Radius.circular(20.0),),
 ),
)
```

Figure 15-7. *BorderRadius on all four corners*

BoxShape

Your containers don't have to always be rectangles. When you need it to be another shape, you can make it so with BoxShape or CustomPainter. BoxShape is much easier to use, but it only supports circles, as in Figure 15-8 (in addition to the default rectangle, of course):

```
Container(
  decoration: BoxDecoration(
    shape: BoxShape.circle,
    color: Colors.deepOrange,
  ),
),
```

Figure 15-8. *BoxShape.circle makes your Container round*

CustomPainter is way more complex, but it allows infinite shapes. It would be distracting to get too deep into the details of CustomPainter (Figure 15-9), but here's a quick example, a Superman shield:

```
Container(
  child: CustomPaint(
    size: Size(200, 200),
    painter: SupermanShieldPainter(),
```

```
  ),
)
class SupermanShieldPainter extends CustomPainter {
  @override
  void paint(Canvas canvas, Size size) {
    canvas.drawPath(Path()
    ..moveTo(25, 0)
    ..lineTo(125, 0)
    ..lineTo(150,25)
    ..lineTo(75, 125)
    ..lineTo(0,25)
    ..lineTo(25,0),
    Paint()
    ..style=PaintingStyle.fill
    ..color = Colors.red
    );
  }
  @override
  bool shouldRepaint(oldDelegate) => false;
}
```

Figure 15-9. *Using a CustomPainter*

See? Quite a bit more involved. Note that your container is still a rectangle. It's just that the background is different. To dive deeper into CustomPainter, take a look at `https://api.flutter.dev/flutter/widgets/CustomPaint-class.html`.

Tip   All of these decorations are applied to the decoration property, but they can also apply to a property called foregroundDecoration which, as the name suggests, is applied on a layer *above* the container. Because they're drawn on top of the other things, you'll want to keep in mind one more modification: opacity. Colors can be made semitransparent. The following would create a red layer on top of a container that is 50% transparent:

```
foregroundDecoration: BoxDecoration(
  color:Colors.red.withOpacity(0.5),
),
```

Conclusion

In many ways, the Container is the quintessential Flutter widget, allowing tons of options to fine-tune your layouts. Heck, you could do the whole thing with Containers because they're so versatile! (Don't actually do this, kids. We're just talking theory here.) But Containers are spectacularly useful for fine-tuning layouts and for adding visual decorations to so many other widgets.

Hey, congratulations! You made it through some very tough concepts, all of which we hope were made easier to learn in the last few chapters. We're going to finish off the book with a related subject: special presentational widgets. These will take your layouts to the next level!

CHAPTER 16

Layout – Special Presentation Widgets

After the prior five chapters on layout, we've now covered the tools you'll need for 90% of your layout needs, but there are more. A few are worth a glance just so you know what tool to reach for should the situation come up. These widgets are designed for very particular layout situations that, while common, aren't everyday but need specialized tools to make happen.

We're going to glance at Slivers and then do deep dives into Stack and Table widgets.

Slivers

Slivers are a major topic, enough for a couple more chapters so we'll stay surfacy. Our goal will be awareness. If you know what they're good for that'll suffice for now. Slivers are for customized scrolling designs.

You may someday have need to create parallax effects, or sections collapsing when they're at the top but scrolling when they're in view, or multiple ListViews that scroll but you can also scroll between them, or scrollable lists that have subheadings, or widgets where you can scroll inside something that is also scrollable itself. Slivers enable these advanced scrolling behaviors. Kind of mind-blowing, right?

© Rap Payne 2024
R. Payne, *Flutter App Development*, https://doi.org/10.1007/979-8-8688-0485-4_16

Let's just bottom-line it like this: when the regular Flutter widgets aren't enough to meet your out-of-the-box scrolling needs, Slivers can help. Slivers are *scrollable portions* of a screen. These are your major Sliver widgets:

- SliverList – Like ListView, but with more flexibility for custom scroll effects

- SliverFixedExtentList – Similar to SliverList but keeps all children at a fixed size for grids or lists with uniform items

- SliverAppBar – An app bar that can collapse or expand as the user scrolls

- SliverPadding – Adds scrolling-aware padding to a sliver element

- SliverGrid – Renders a grid layout within the scrollable area

And if none of those are exactly what you want, perhaps try building your own custom scrollable widget, extending the Sliver class and overriding layoutChild and similar methods.

Stack Widget

This is for when you want to layer widgets so that they occupy the same X- and Y-position on the screen, overlapping one another. You want to … well … *stack* them in the Z-direction. With Stack, you'll list some number of subwidgets, and they'll be displayed in that order one on top of another. The last one will occult (hide) the previous one which will occult the one before that and so on.

Using a Stack, you can create some really cool layouts. In fact, Material Cards rely on Stacks a lot because they embrace background images with text on top of it. Maybe we want a card with a person's profile pic with their name and info superimposed on top (Figure 16-1). [1]

Figure 16-1. *A Card with text on top of an image thanks to a Stack widget*

Here's how we might accomplish that:

```
Card(
 child: Stack(
  children: <Widget>[
   Image.asset("sandeep.jpg"),
   Column(
    children: <Widget>[
     Text("Sandeep Patel", style: _bigText),
     Expanded(child: Container()), // For the gap
     Text("Email: s.patel@us.com"),
     Text("Phone: +1 (555) 786-3512"),
    ],
   ),
```

[1] Images for Figures 16-1 through 16-3 courtesy Hosein Hakimi on Unsplash.com

```
    ],
  ),
),
```

In the Stack, we placed an image first. Then on top of that, we added a Column with text elements. Since the Column was added *after* the image, it appears in front of the image.

Positioned Widget

In our preceding example, the texts laid out decently because a Column centers its children and the Expanded pushed the Texts to the top and bottom. But if we just had everything directly in the Stack, it would look like Figure 16-2.

Figure 16-2. *Without a Positioned widget, everything bunches up in the upper left*

When you use a Stack, every widget inside it will try to stay in the top-left corner. We can accurately place those inner widgets in a Stack anywhere we want by wrapping them in a Positioned widget.[2]

---

[2] There are other techniques to position inside of a Stack such as Container, Align, and Padding. But Position works great with Stack.

```
Card(
 child: Stack(
  children: <Widget>[
   Image.asset("sandeep.jpg"),
   Positioned(
    top: 10, left: 10,
    child: Text("Sandeep Patel", style: _bigText),
   ),
   Positioned(
    bottom: 30, right: 10,
    child: Text("Email: s.patel@us.com",),
   ),
   Positioned(
    bottom: 10, right: 10,
    child: Text("Phone: +1 (555) 786-3512",),
   ),
   Positioned(
    bottom: 0, left: 0, height: 100, width: 100,
    child: FlutterLogo(),
   ),
  ],
 ),
),
```

We threw in a FlutterLogo for good measure. It now looks like Figure 16-3. Much nicer!

Figure 16-3. *Much nicer looking with a Positioned widget*

The Positioned widget makes its child a fixed distance from one of the four corners by specifying the top, bottom, left, and/or right positions.

Card Widget

You may have noticed that we used a Card widget in our preceding example. A Card feels like the right thing to do in this situation, but it is by no means required.

A Flutter Card widget was created to implement the Material Design look and feel, having properties like *color* for the background, *elevation* for a drop shadow size, *borderOnForeground* for the border, and *margin* for spacing around it. Granted, all of those could also be accomplished with a Container. But if you want to do it with a standard look and feel, a Card makes it easy:

```
Card(
  elevation: 20.0,
  child: Text("This is text in a card",),
),
```

The Table Widget

The GridView is great when displaying widgets in Rows and Columns that wrap. The wrapping part means that you really don't care which children widgets end up in which Row and Column. Location means nothing. You just want them to appear neatly.

Rows and Columns are best when you *do* care in which Row and Column each child exists. They're rigid when you want them to be. Unfortunately, the columns can't talk to each other so they will often be misaligned (Figures 16-4 and 16-5).

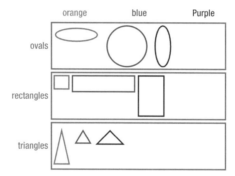

Figure 16-4. *Rows with nested widgets work but the columns are misaligned*

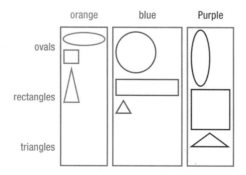

Figure 16-5. *Columns with nested widgets work but the rows are misaligned*

The Table widget fixes that problem. It is rigid like nested Rows and Columns, but each Row and Column is aware of the others and lines up nicely (Figure 16-6).

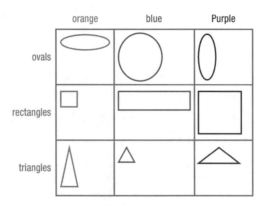

Figure 16-6. *A Table aligns the rows and columns*

A Table widget will have children, a list of TableRow widgets. And each TableRow widget will have children, a list of subwidgets:

```
return Table(
 children: [
  // Row #1, the header row
  TableRow(children: [
    Text('Salesperson', style: _bold,),
    Text('January', style: _bold,),
    Text('February', style: _bold,),
    Text('March', style: _bold,),
   ]
  ),
  // Row #2
  TableRow(children: [
    Text('Dwight'),
```

```
    Text('3742'),
    Text('5573'),
    Text('4323'),
   ],
  ),
  // Row #3
  TableRow(children: [
    Text('Phyllis'),
    Text('3823'),
    Text('4500'),
    Text('3277'),
   ],
  ),
 ],
);
```

The preceding code would produce Figure 16-7.

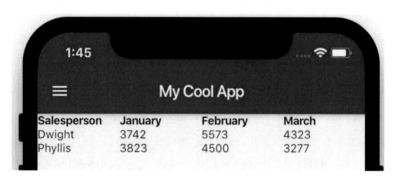

Figure 16-7. *A Table widget lines up Rows and Columns simultaneously*

Caution   Anyone coming from an HTML background knows that laying out a page using HTML <table>s is possible but a bad idea. <table>s are for data, not for layout. Well, it's the same thing in Flutter. It is possible, but generally speaking, stay away from tables for laying out a page. But if you have data, Tables are the right choice.

If you want more control over the Column widths, set the columnWidths property to a Map of Column number to width. The following would give the first column 30% of the width and divide the remaining 70% evenly across the remaining columns:

```
return Table(
 columnWidths: {0: FractionColumnWidth(0.3)},
 children: <TableRow>[ ...
```

How do you span Columns? Like for a table header, for example. Unfortunately, you don't with Flutter Table – yet. Maybe someday. There is a feature request for spanning columns.

Conclusion

Flutter's rich and varied selection of widgets is simultaneously a strength and contributor to much confusion – a mixed bag for sure. After this, our sixth (!) chapter on layout widgets, you've surely got enough information to solve most layout problems you'll come across. In this chapter in particular, we've covered some unusual layout widgets, giving you power to create some very imaginative Flutter screens.

Thanks for joining me on this journey! I wish you all the best on your Flutter endeavors!

Dart Language Overview

We use the Dart language when writing Flutter, but Dart isn't very popular (yet). Most developers jump right into Flutter with no prior knowledge of the language. In case that's you, we wanted to get you a little assistance.

In this appendix, we're making no attempt to teach you everything about Dart. Our goal here is to get you juuuuuust enough Dart to be effective as you write Flutter. So this appendix is brief and to the point. We are only dealing with the things that would otherwise have slowed you down while writing Flutter. An example of this is the *rune* data type. Super cool and innovative Dart feature, but rarely used with Flutter so we omitted it. Please try to be tolerant of us if we left out your favorite feature. We didn't forget it. We just decided it wasn't as important as you thought it should be.

What Is Dart?

Dart is a compiled, statically typed, object-oriented, procedural programming language. It has a very mainstream structure much like other OO languages, making it awfully easy to pick up for folks who have experience with Java, C#, C++, or other OO, C-like languages. And it adds some features that developers in those other languages would not expect but are very cool nonetheless and make the language more than elegant.

In light of all that, we've organized this appendix in two sections:

- Expected Features – A quick reference (a.k.a. a "cheat sheet") of mainstream features, the bare minimum of what you'll need to know for Flutter. You should tear through this section at lightning speed.

- Unexpected Features – These are things that might be a surprise to developers who work in traditional OO languages. Since Dart departs from tradition in these areas, we thought it best to explain them briefly – very briefly.

Expected Features – Dart Cheat Sheet

This quick reference assumes that you're an experienced OO developer and ignores the stuff that would be painfully obvious to you. For a more in-depth and detailed look at Dart, please visit `https://dart.dev/guides/language/language-tour`.

Data Types

```
int x = 10;           // Integers
double y = 2.0;       // IEEE754 floating point numbers
bool z = true;        // Booleans
String s = "hello";   // Strings
dynamic d;            // Dynamic variables can change types
d = x;                // at any time. Use sparingly!
d = y;
d = z;
```

Arrays/Lists

```dart
// Square brackets means a list/array
// In Dart, arrays and lists are the same thing.
List<dynamic> list = [1, "two", 3];
// Dart supports Generics
// Optional angle brackets set the type

// How to iterate a list
for (var d in list) {
  print(d);
}

// Another way to iterate a list
list.forEach((d) => print(d));
// Both of these would print "1", then "two", then "3"
```

Conditional Expressions

```dart
// Traditional if/else statement
int x = 10;
if (x < 100) {
  print('Yes');
} else {
  print('No');
}
// Would print "Yes"

// Dart also supports ternaries
String response = (x < 100) ? 'Yes' : 'No';
```

Looping

```
// A for loop
for (int i=1 ; i<10 ; i++) {
  print(i);
}
// Would print 1 thru 9

// A while loop
int i=1;
while (i<10) {
  print(i++);
}
// Would print 1 thru 9
```

Classes

```
class Name {
  String first='';
  String last='';
  String suffix='';
}
class Person {
 // Classes have properties
 int id='';
 Name name = new Name();// Another class can be used as a type
 String email;
 String phone;
 // Classes have methods
 void save() {
    // Write to a database somehow.
 }
}
```

Class Constructors

```
class Person {
  Name name;
  // Typical constructor
  Person() {
    name = Name();
    name.first = "";
    name.last = "";
  }
}
```

Unexpected Things About Dart

The preceding Dart features were unsurprising to any experienced OO developers, but Dart has some pretty cool features that are unique. We'll cover these next, but since they're less familiar, let's take just a sentence or two for each and explain it briefly before giving you a code sample.

Type Inference

If I said "x=10.0," what data type would you guess that x is? Double? And how did you know? Because you looked to the right of the equal sign and *inferred* its type based upon the value being assigned to it. Dart can do that too. If you use the keyword var instead of a data type, Dart will infer what type it is and assign that type:

```
var i = 10;          // i is now defined as an int.
i = 12;              // Works, because 12 is an int.
i = "twelve";        // No! "twelve" is a String, not an int.
```

```
var str = "ten";       // str is now defined as a String.
str = "a million";   // Yep, works great.
str = 1000000.0;     // Nope! That's a double, not a string.
```

This is often confused with dynamic. Dynamic can hold any data type and can change at runtime. Using dynamic is dangerous and should be discouraged. Var is strongly and statically typed.

In summary

- dynamic – Can store any data type. The data type can change at any time.

- var – The data type is inferred from the value on the right side of the "=". The data type does not change.

final vs. const

final and const are Dart variable modifiers:

```
final int x = 10;
const double y = 2.0;
```

They both mean that once assigned, the value can't change. But const goes a little farther – the value is set at compile time and is therefore embedded in the installation bundle.

final means that the variable can't be reassigned. It does not mean that it can't change. For example, this is allowed:

```
final Employee e = Employee();
e.employer = "The Bluth Company";
```

e changed, but it wasn't reassigned so that's okay. This, however, is not allowed:

```
e = Employee('Different','person');
```

final marks a *variable* as unchangeable, but const marks a *value* as unchangeable.

In summary

- final – The variable, once set, cannot be reassigned.

- const – The value is set at compile time, not runtime.

Null Safety

Dart has *sound null safety*. This just means that it protects you from accidentally using a null value in a way that would cause runtime errors. For example, if you declared what you thought was an object but was in fact a null and then tried to access a member. That's a null exception. Your dart code won't compile if that's possible.

Dart demands that variables can never hold a null value unless you purposely mark it as nullable. The compiler and linter will diligently look for any violations and tell you about them.

To mark a variable as nullable, put a question mark ("?") after the data type:

```
int? x;
double? y;
bool? z;
String? name;
Person? p;
```

All of the preceding data are null since they haven't been assigned a value yet. At runtime, you must handle possible null values:

```
print(name);    // This will not compile. name may be null.
print(name ?? 'No name given');   // Cool! There's a fallback
print(p.age);   // Nope! p might be null.
```

```
print(p?.age);  // Good. If p is null, we return null.
print(p!.age);  // Allows it to compile but if p is null
                // here, it throws at runtime. That's bad! Use
                // "!" only when you know p cannot be null.
```

String interpolationwith $

Interpolation saves devs from writing string concatenations. This …

```
String fullName = '$first $last, $suffix';
```

… is effectively the same thing as this …

```
String fullName = first + " " + last + ", " + suffix;
```

When the variable is part of a map or an object, the compiler can get confused, so you should wrap the interpolation in curly braces.

```
String fullName = '${name['first']} ${name['last']}';
```

Multiline Strings

You can create multiline strings with three single or double quotes:

```
String introduction = """
Now the story of a wealthy family
who lost everything
And the one son who had no choice
but to keep them all together.
""";
```

Spread Operator

The ".." operator will spread out the elements of an array, flattening them. This will be very familiar to JavaScript developers:

```
List fiveTo10 = [ 5, 6, 7, 8, 9, 10, ];
// Spreading the inner array with "...":
List numbers = [ 1, 2, 3, 4, ...fiveTo10, 11, 12];
// numbers now has [1, 2, 3, 4, 5, 6, 7, 8, 9, 10, 11, 12]
```

Map<foo, bar>

Maps are like a hash or dictionary. They're merely an object with a set of key–value pairs. The keys and values can be of any type:

```
// You set the value of a Map with curly braces:
Map<String, dynamic> person = {
  "first": "George",
  "last": "Bluth",
  "dob": DateTime.parse("1972-07-16"),
  "email": "amazingGob@gmail.com",
};
// Angle brackets on a Map set the data types of the keys and
// values. They're not required but are a good practice
// You reference a map member with square brackets:
String intro = "${person['first']} was born ${person['dob']}";
```

Functions Are Objects

Just like in JavaScript, functions are first-class objects. They can be passed around like data, returned from a function, passed into a function as a parameter, or set equal to a variable. You can do just about anything with a function that you can do with an object in Java or C#:

```
Function sayHi = (String name) => print("Hello, $name");
// You can pass sayHi around like data; it's an object!
Function meToo = sayHi;
meToo("Tobias");
```

Big Arrow/Fat Arrow/Lambda

In the preceding example, we also saw the fat arrow syntax. When you have a function that returns a value in one line of code, you can put that returned value on the right side of a "=>" and the argument list on the left side. These are all the same:

```
int triple(int val) {
  return val * 3;
}
Function triple = (int val) {
  return val * 3;
};
Function triple = (int val) => val * 3;
```

The fat arrow is just syntactic sugar, allowing devs to be more expressive with less code.

Named Function Parameters

Positional parameters are great, but it can be less error prone (albeit more typing) to have named parameters. Instead of calling a function like this:

```
sendEmail('ceo@bluthcompany.com','Popcorn in the breakroom');
```

You can call it like this:

```
sendEmail(subject:'Popcorn in the breakroom',
  toAddress:'ceo@bluthcompany.com');
```

Now, the order of parameters is unimportant. Here is how you'd write the function to use named parameters. Note the curly braces:

```
void sendEmail({String toAddress, String subject}) {
  // send the email here
}
```

Named parameters also work great with class constructors where they are very commonly used in Flutter:

```
class Person {
  Name name;
  // Named parameters
  Person({String firstName, String lastName}) {
    name = Name()..first=firstName..last=lastName;
  }
}
```

Omitting "new" and "this."

In Dart, it is possible – and encouraged – to avoid the use of the *new* keyword when instantiating a class:

```
// No. Avoid.
Person p = new Person();
// Yes
Person p = Person();
```

In the same way, inside of a class, the use of "this." to refer to members of the class is not only unneeded because it is assumed, but it is also discouraged. The code is shorter and cleaner:

```
class Name {
 String first;
 String last;
```

```
String suffix;
String getFullName() {
 // No. Avoid "this.":
 String full=this.first+" "+this.last+", "+this.suffix;
 // Better.
 String full=first+" "+last+", "+suffix;
 return full;
}
}
```

Class Constructor Parameter Shorthand

Merely a shorter way of writing your Dart classes, when you write the constructor to receive "this.something" and have a class-scoped property with the same name, the compiler writes the assignments so you don't have to.

```
class Person {
  String email;
  String phone;
  // The parameters are assigned to properties automatically
  // because the parameters say "this."
  Person(this.email, this.phone) {}
}
```

The preceding code is equivalent to

```
class Person {
  String email;
  String phone;
  Person(String email, String phone) {
    this.email = email;
```

```
    this.phone = phone;
  }
}
```

Private Class Members

Dart does not use class visibility modifiers such as public, private, protected, package, or friend like other OO languages. All members are public by default. To make a class member private, put an underscore in front of the name:

```
class Person {
  int id;
  String email;
  String phone;
  String _password;
  set password(String value) {
    _password = value;
  }
  String get hashedPassword {
    return sha512.convert(utf8.encode(_password)).toString();
  }
}
```

In that example, id, email, and phone are public. _password is private because the first character in the name is "_", the underscore character.

Mixins

Mixins are baskets of properties and methods that can be added to any class. They look like classes but cannot be instantiated:

```
mixin Employment {
  String employer;
  String businessPhone;
  void callBoss() {
    print('Calling my boss');
  }
}
```

A mixin is added to a class when it uses the "with" keyword:

```
class Employee extends Person with Employment {
  String position;
}
```

This Employee class now has employer and businessPhone properties and a callBoss() method:

```
Employee e = Employee();
e.employer = "The Bluth Company";
e.callBoss();        // An employee can call its boss.
```

Dart, like Java and C#, only supports single inheritance. A class can only extend one thing. But mixin members are added to a class so any class can implement multiple mixins and a mixin can be used in multiple other classes.

The Cascade Operator (..)

When you see two dots, it means "return this class, but before you do, do something with a property or method." We might do this

```
Person p = Person()..id=100..email='gob@bluth.com'..save();
```

which would be a more concise way of writing

```
Person p = Person();
p.id=100;
p.email='gob@bluth.com';
p.save();
```

No Overloading

Dart does not support overloading methods. This includes constructors.

Named Constructors

Since we can't have overloaded constructors, Dart supports a different way of doing essentially the same thing. They're called named constructors and they happen when you write a typical constructor, but you tack on a dot and another name:

```
class Person {
  // Typical constructor
  Person() {
    name = Name()..first=""..last="";
  }
  // A named constructor
  Person.byName({String first, String last}) {
    name = Name()
      ..first = firstName
      ..last = lastName;
  }
  // Another named constructor
  Person.byId(int id) {
    // Maybe go fetch from a service by the provided id
  }
}
```

And to use these named constructors, do this:

```
Person p = Person();
// p would be a person with a blank first and last name
Person p1 = Person.byName(first:"Lindsay",last:"Fünke");
// p1 has a first name of "Lindsay" and a last name of "Funke"
Person p2 = Person.byId(100);
// p2 would be fetched based on the id of 100
```

Futures, Async, and Await

Flutter is written using Dart. Dart is a single-threaded language. So Flutter apps are single-threaded. This means that a Flutter app can only do one thing at a time.

That is all true. But that does *not* mean that Flutter apps are forced to wait for slower processes.

Flutter Apps Use an Event Loop

This should come as no surprise since Android has a main looper and iOS has a run loop (a.k.a. main loop). Heck, even JavaScript devs are unimpressed since JavaScript itself has a … wait for it … event loop. Yes, all the cool kids are using an event loop these days.

An event loop is a background infinite loop which periodically wakes up and looks in the event queue for any tasks that need to run. If any exist, the event loop puts them onto the run stack if and only if the CPU is idle.

As your app is running instructions, they run serially – one after another. If an instruction is encountered that may potentially block the main thread waiting on some resource, it is started and the "wait" part is put on a separate queue.

R. Payne, *Flutter App Development*, https://doi.org/10.1007/979-8-8688-0485-4

Why Would It Wait?

Certain things are slow compared to the CPU. Reading from a file is slow. Writing to a file is even slower. Communicating via Ajax? Forget about it. If we kept the waiting activity on the main thread, it would block all other activities. What a waste!

The way this is handled in JavaScript, iOS, Android, and now Dart is this:

1. An activity that is well known to be slow is started up as normal.

2. The moment it begins waiting for something – disk, HTTP request, whatever – it is moved away from the CPU.

3. A listener of sorts is created. Its job is to monitor the activity and raises an event when it is finished waiting.

4. The reference to that listener is returned to the main thread. This reference object is known as a *Future*.

5. The main thread continues chugging along its merry way.

6. When the waiting activity is finally resolved, the event loop sees it and runs an associated method on the main thread to handle finishing up the slow event.

All you do is write the code to create the future and to handle futures that are returned from other methods.

```
// Say goReadAFile() is slow and returns a Future
Future myFuture = goReadAFile();
```

In Dart, you have the ability to specify the type of thing that Future will give you eventually.

Table B-1. *Futures and their types.*

Type of future	When it's ready, I'll have a ...
Future<String>	... String
Future<Foo>	... Foo
Future<Map<String, dynamic>>	... Map whose keys are Strings and whose values are dynamic.

When we have that Future object, you may not have the data, but you definitely have a promise to get that data in the Future. (See what they did there?)

How Do We Get the Data from a Future?

You tell the Future what to do once the data is ready. Basically, you're responding to a "Yo, the data is ready" event and telling the Future what to do by registering a function which we refer to as a *callback*.

```
myFuture.then(myCallback);
```

The .then() function is how you register that callback function. The callback should be written to handle the promised data. For example, if we have a Future<Foo> then our callback should have this signature:

```
void myCallback(Foo theIncomingData) {
 doSomethingWith(theIncomingData);
}
```

So if the Future will return a Person, your callback should **receive** a Person. If the Future promises a String, your callback should receive a String. And so forth.

About the return value: if your callbacks return a value, that value will be wrapped in a new Future. The returned value isn't available to your main function. This makes a ton of sense when you think about it because remember that it is no longer running within the main thread of your app so it has no way of merging back in. So how do you get a value from the callback? Several methods, but the most understandable is that you use a variable that is defined outside the callback:

```
class FooState extends State<FooComponent> {
  String _first;  // <-- A variable known by the whole class
  Widget build(BuildContext context) {
    // return a widget
  }
  void _myCallback(String someVar) {
    _first = someVar;  // <- Getting a value OUT of a callback
  }
}
```

To get a value out of an async callback, you set an external variable.

Tacking a .then() onto your Future object can occasionally muddy up your code. If you prefer, you can clean it up a bit with *await*.

Await

There's another way to get the data which is more straightforward for other devs to understand. Instead of using .then(), you can *await* the data.

```
Foo theIncomingData = await somethingThatReturnsAFuture();
```

Awaiting pauses the running code to ... well ... wait for the Future to resolve before it moves on to the next line. In the example above, the "Foo" that you're awaiting is returned and put into theIncomingData. Simple.

Or maybe it isn't that simple...

Async

Like it or not, when you use await inside a function, that function is now in danger of blocking the main thread, so it must be marked as async. For example, this function ...

```
Bar someFunction() {
  Foo theIncomingData = someFunction();
  return new Bar();
}
```

... becomes this when we await:

```
Future<Bar> someFunction() async {
  Foo theIncomingData = await somethingThatReturnsAFuture();
  return new Bar();
}
```

Note that when we added an await on line 2, we **must** mark the function itself with async. The subtle thing is that when it is marked as async, anything returned from that function is immediately wrapped in a Future unless it is already one.

Are you sitting down? Check this out: Whenever you choose to await a future, the function must be marked as async and therefore all who call it must be awaited and they must be marked as async and so on and so on. Eventually you get to a high enough spot in the call chain that you're not in a function so you don't have to mark it as async.

Maybe I spoke too soon when I said this is simpler.

Hint   The Flutter build() method cannot be async but events like onPress can. So try to steer your async activities into events to solve this recursive async–await–async–await thing.

Summary

Here are your takeaways:

1. Futures allow your Dart code to be asynchronous – it can handle slow-running processes in a separate thread (kind of).

2. You can handle the callbacks of those things with either a .then(callback) or by awaiting them.

3. If you await in a function, that function must be marked as async.

If you'd like to do some more reading on Futures, here's a thorough coverage from the Dart team: `www.dartlang.org/tutorials/language/ futures`.

APPENDIX C

Including Packages in Your Flutter App

Every day, Flutter developers across the globe will run into situations that have already been solved by others. They'll use a packaged library to solve it and they'll get that library at no cost in seconds from `https://pub.dev` by running a couple of simple commands.

Over the years, community-minded developers like you and me have created and packaged libraries for other developers to use in their Flutter apps. Once a problem has been solved, these developers will take certain steps to package their code and upload it to pub.dev so that you and I can discover it, download it, and include it into our Flutter apps to solve the same problems. They do not get paid to do this. They do it merely out of the kindness of their hearts. Well, that and the prestige that comes from having published a popular library.

Finding a Library to Use

Oftentimes, you'll know which library you need because you'll be told which one to get. This is nice because you don't need to search for one. At other times, you're in the middle of writing a Flutter app, solving a particular problem and you suddenly think, "Surely someone has published a solution to this at pub.dev." When that happens, point your favorite browser at `https://pub.dev`. You'll see a search bar at the top like in Figure C-1.

R. Payne, *Flutter App Development*, https://doi.org/10.1007/979-8-8688-0485-4

277

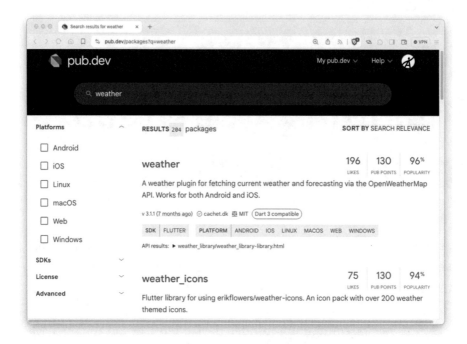

Figure C-1. *A pub.dev search result for "weather"*

Put in a keyword or two and click the search button. The search capability on pub.dev is surprisingly effective. Its results will usually include dozens or maybe hundreds of results. Just scroll, click on some options that look promising, and read up on it. Keep narrowing down until you find the best option. It may not take long at all.

Tip   Each library has a popularity which measures how many downloads of this package have occurred. This is sort of a proxy for community endorsement; the more of us have downloaded this package, the more likely it is to have solved our problems. I use it to hint at which are more reliable and which might be kind of sketchy.

I'm probably going to go with the second of the results in Figure C-2.

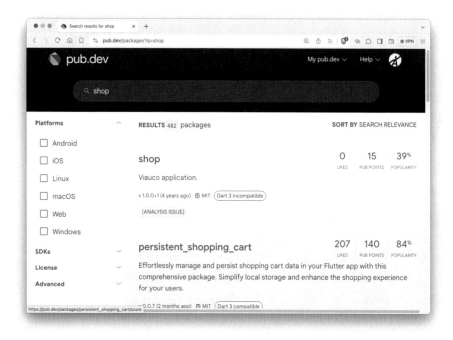

Figure C-2. *Each package's popularity hints at how successful others have been with it*

If the built-in search functionality doesn't do it for you, ask around. Reddit has subreddits dedicated to Flutter; there is a discord channel and Slack groups you can join full of Flutter devs who can lend their expertise in helping you locate the perfect library. And if it doesn't exist, consider publishing your own. Instructions for that are as follows.

Downloading the Library

Once you've located the perfect library, make note of its name. Open a terminal window in your project's directory and run

```
flutter pub add <package_name>
```

This will retrieve the library package from pub.dev and install it on your machine in a folder in your home directory called .pub_cache. .pub_cache holds the only copy of that library across your entire machine. Your Flutter project will have a .dart_tool folder containing symbolic links to your .pub_cache folder so it knows where to find the actual dart source code to include when compiling.

This `flutter pub add` command will also add the installed package and version to your pubspec.yaml file.

The pubspec.yaml File

Located in your project's root, this is the configuration file for your project. It holds information about your project, including dependencies – packages like the one above that your project depends upon:

```
name: my_project
description: A demonstration Flutter application
version: 3.4.12+1
environment:
  sdk: '>=A.B.C <X.Y.Z'
dependencies:
  flutter:
    sdk: flutter
  intl: ^A.B.C
  http: ^1.2.3
dev_dependencies:
  flutter_test:
    sdk: flutter
flutter:
  uses-material-design: true
  assets:
    - assets/daam.png
```

Do your recognize the format? It is YAML format. You can get the official specs for YAML format at `https://yaml.org/spec/1.2.2/`, but it is clearly key–value pairs with indentation being very important.

Most of the keys are self-explanatory, but I'm going to touch on a couple that may not be obvious.

- Version uses SEMVER (`https://semver.org/`).

- Environment tells us what version of the Flutter SDK this project needs. The version installed on this machine must be A.B.C or greater and less than X.Y.Z.

- The dependencies section tells us that our project needs the flutter, intl, and http packages. The carat (^) character means that if we update our versions, we cannot go beyond the major number. For example, in the http package above, we may update to 1.4 or 1.37, but never 2.0 because a change in the major number expects there to be breaking changes.

Using These Packages in Your Code

When you run `flutter pub add`, the needed package is downloaded to your machine and pointed to in your pubspec.yaml file. All that's left is to import it into your code. In every dart source code file where a piece of that library package is needed, you'll add an import statement.

To import the entire package:

```
import 'package:foo/foo.dart';
```

This is the simplest and most common import. It'll be used most often. But there are some other handy techniques.

To import parts of the package:

```
import 'package:foo/foo.dart' show bar;
```

Showing will only expose those members that you're explicitly listing. It's a little extra typing but is obvious and maybe the best practice. It prevents accidental name collisions. Speaking of which …

To import the package but rename it:

```
import 'package:foo/foo.dart' as baz;
```

This is handy if you have two libraries with similarly named members. This will prevent name collisions because you'd refer to one as baz. methodName and the other as just methodName (or whatever).

Keeping Your Packages Current

Some packages may have new versions from their authors. To find out which have new versions go:

```
flutter pub outdated
```

Caution   Just because a package is outdated doesn't mean there's anything wrong with it. Downloading a new version may actually break things in your code. Don't download gratuitously. Only do it when there's a new feature you want or they've fixed a bug.

Then to update packages, edit pubspec.yaml, changing the version to the latest. Then run

```
flutter pub get
```

This will read your new pubspec.yaml and install the newer version.

How to Upload Your Own Library

Maybe you've created a cool tool and want to share it. It's not too tough to upload a library for others. Here's how.

1. **Pick a unique package name, one that hasn't already been taken on pub.dev.**

   Just go to pub.dev and keep searching on your preferred package names until you find one that is unique. If a package exists, it will be found at `https://pub.dev/packages/<package_name>`.

2. **On your development machine, create a package project.**

   Use flutter create with the --template=package flag to create your new project:

   ```
   flutter create --template=package <package_name>
   ```

   Obviously, what you're making is not a typical Flutter app. There is no main() to run and no full-screen scenes to view. This template will create the wrapper for uploading into pub.dev.

3. **Write your code.**

   Write your Dart code in the lib folder, with all the usual classes, functions, and widgets.

   You probably will want to run `flutter analyze` and `flutter format` on your code because once it's public, other developers will savage you on X/Twitter if your code isn't perfect. ☺

4. **Edit** pubspec.yaml **with ...**

- Name – Your package's unique name

- Description – One sentence explanation of what it does

- Version – The initial version number (e.g. 1.0.0)

- Repository – A link to your repo like GitHub and where issues with your package can be reported

- Homepage – An optional link to your website where further detailed information on usage may be found

- Environment – The flutter and SDK versions it needs

- Dependencies – Any external packages your code needs

5. **Write a README.md, CHANGELOG.md, and LICENSE.**

Your README.md is in markdown format and also allows some limited HTML formatting.

You probably want to include

- Installation instructions

- Usage examples

- Contribution guidelines

Your CHANGELOG.md is also in markdown format but is much simpler. This is where you'll list each version, date, and what changed in that version from the prior, especially breaking changes. And out of kindness to your fellow developers, make sure you're using semantic versioning (SEMVER).

Choose a standard legal license (e.g. MIT, Apache, BSD) or write your own. Put it in a file called LICENSE. Yes, all caps and no extension.

6. **Publish your package.**

- In a browser, sign in to pub.dev using a Google account.

- On your development machine, run `flutter pub publish` to upload your package.

- Follow the prompts to authenticate and confirm publishing.

7. **Wait for pub.dev review.**

The pub.dev team will look over your code to make sure there's nothing malicious about it. Once they're comfortable, they'll approve it. At this point, your package is available for anyone to download and install via `flutter pub add <package_name>`.

8. **Enjoy the fruits of your labor and the riches, fame, and power that will certainly ensue.**

Just kidding, you'll probably get nothing except the satisfaction of having helped others. That, and maybe some geek cred for having published a Flutter package. Seriously, give a talk on how you did it. Tweet it, put it on Reddit, Slack, Discord, whatever. And for sure put it on your CV/resume.

APPENDIX D

How to Work with Files

At this point in our journey, you've learned how to create a Flutter app and precisely control how it looks and lays out in any orientation and on any device. That's pretty cool! You know how to have it maintain data with Form fields. But how do we get it to save that data? How do we get it to read that data in the first place?

Your app's data can only come from three sources: from the user, from within the device itself, or by exchanging data with an external server. You can read about getting data from the user in Chapter 4, "Value Widgets," and about external servers in Chapter 9, "Making RESTful API Calls with HTTP." In this appendix, let's learn to read and write data from on-device storage options. Here will be our plan for the appendix:

- Bundling files in your app
- Reading/writing a local file
- Converting JSON
- Saving user preferences

© Rap Payne 2024
R. Payne, *Flutter App Development*, https://doi.org/10.1007/979-8-8688-0485-4

Including a File with Your App

The file you're trying to read must exist (duh). Maybe we should just manually create one.

It isn't uncommon at all for developers to package up a flat file that should be installed along with your app. It is great for initializations of larger amounts of data – kind of like a mini database. It should look familiar because this is the same technique we used to bundle images with our app. All you'll do is create the file in your IDE and reference it in pubspec.yaml.

There are a dozen ways to add the file to your project. Use a command prompt, right-click and choose "new" in your IDE, drag and drop in file explorer, and so on. But in the end, it should be visible in your IDE.

It is common but not required to create it in a folder called assets (Figure D-1).

Figure D-1. *"assets" folder*

But even though it exists, the app is unaware of a file until we flag it in pubspec.yaml. Put it in the assets section of pubspec.yaml, and it will be included with the .ipa/.apk for installation on devices:

```
# To add assets to your app, add an assets section, like this:
assets:
  - assets/database.json
```

To read that file, you'll use rootBundle.loadString() like this:

```
try {
  String data =
      await rootBundle.loadString('assets/database.json');
  debugPrint(data);
} catch (e) {
  print('Error: $e');
  rethrow;
}
```

rootBundle is part of services.dart, so make sure you import it.

```
import 'package:flutter/services.dart';
```

Tip   If the assets file is structured with keys and values, the rootBundle.loadStructuredData(key, function) method may be a better choice. It allows you to pass in the key you're reading and a function to process the data being read.

Since this data is written at compile time on the development machine, it can't be changed. But we can create a file in our app's documents folder that can be read and written. Let's look at that next.

Writing a File

Sometimes our users want to save values from one run to another. We can allow that in a local file, one that exists on their device. To create a file, you can simply write to it with myFile.writeAsString(theString). But our app can't just write to any location on the device. We have to get a reference to a writeable directory which is exactly what the path_provider library does (https://pub.dev/packages/path_provider). It has a method called getApplicationDocumentsDirectory() which returns a Future<Directory>. So if we await that call, we can get a directory and create a file in it:

```
// Get the documents directory
Directory docs = await getApplicationDocumentsDirectory();
// Write the file
try {
  File file = File('${docs.path}/$_filename');
  await file.writeAsString(_someText);
} catch (e) {
  _message = 'Error: $e';
}
```

The Directory and File types are available in Dart's io library. Don't forget to import 'dart:io'.

Caution   For security reasons, writing to a flat file is not possible on the Web.

And Reading It!

Reading a file is even simpler. We just use File.readAsString():

```
File file = File('${docs.path}/$_filename');
file.readAsString().then((text) =>
  setState(() {
    _text = text;
    _message = '$_filename has this text inside it: "$_text"';
  })
```

```
).catchError((e) =>
  setState(() {
    _errorStatus = true;
    _message = 'Error: $e';
  })
);
```

We wanted to use the .then() method of the future here instead of await because the build() method can't be marked as async. The .then() allows you to handle the future without the need for async. Fortunately, the File object also has a readAsStringSync() method which is a blocking call and returns the text directly instead of a Future.

```
try {
  File file = File('${documents.path}/$_filename');
  _text = file.readAsStringSync();
  _message = '$_filename has this text inside it: "$_text"';
} catch (e) {
  _errorStatus = true;
  _message = 'Error: $e';
}
```

Using JSON

When we write files, we're taking something in our app's memory and saving it. Sure, sometimes what we write is just a single value, but very often it is an object or many objects. Let's say we had a list of persons. Maybe the first person in the list is Phoebe Buffay and the second is Rachel Green. If we're going to save this list in a file, we'd have to designate it as a list and specify the properties and values of each person. There are unlimited ways of doing that, but the most popular one is JSON format:

```
{
  "people": [
    {
      "id": "7b5fa0b0-9760-11e9-805d-099f65ed4f55",
      "firstName": "Phoebe",
      "lastName": "Buffay",
      "occupation": "Massage Therapist"
    },
    {
      "id": "110ec58a-a0f2-4ac4-8393-c866d813b8d1",
      "firstName": "Rachel",
      "lastName": "Green",
      "occupation": "Coffee Waitress"
    }
  ]
}
```

Taking data in our app's memory and putting it in that format is called *serializing* the data. Going the other direction, reading data in JSON format, unwrapping it, and loading it into our app's memory is called *deserialization*.

Dart has a built-in library called dart:convert with methods for serializing and deserializing called json.encode() and json.decode(), respectively.

Writing Your App's Memory to JSON

Say your app has an object that you want to store or transmit. To put that data in JSON format, use json.encode(someMap):

```
Map<String, dynamic> jsonMap = {
  "id": _person.id,
  "firstName": _person.firstName,
```

```
  "lastName": _person.lastName,
  "occupation": _person.occupation,
};
try {
  String jsonString = json.encode(jsonMap)
  await file.writeAsString(jsonString);
} catch (e) {
  print("Problem saving! Error: $e");
}
```

Note   A Dart Map is kind of like a JavaScript object: a set of key/value pairs, usually dynamically typed. To get a value, you'd specify a key in square brackets like in the example below. If you want to serialize a strongly typed object, you can either convert it to a map (easier) or implement a method called toJson() which returns a Map (cleaner). toJson() is automatically invoked whenever json.encode is called on an object.

Reading JSON into Your App's Memory

Now let's say you've somehow gotten ahold of a string in JSON format and you want to read that data into your app. How do you deserialize it? json.decode().

```
// jsonString contain serialized JSON data
Map<String, dynamic> personMap = json.decode(jsonString);
// "personMap" is now a Map whose keys are strings
debugPrint(personMap["firstName"]);
Person p = Person(
 id: personMap["id"],
```

```
firstName: person["firstName"],
lastName: person["lastName"],
occupation: person["occupation"]
);
```

Note   jsonEncode( ) is shorthand for json.encode( ). Similarly jsonDecode( ) is shorthand for json.decode( ). It's a stylistic preference. Use whichever you prefer.

You may be thinking about using this technique to store a user's preferences. And sure, it'll totally work. But if you want to save values between runs of the app, there is a better way called *shared preferences*.

Shared Preferences

Most apps will save data locally between runs, settings like authentication tokens, personal data, dark/light modes, sounds ... heck, anything that would be a user preference. On iOS, these things are called NSUserDefaults. On Android, they are called SharedPreferences. And the Flutter team has given us a great library called shared_preferences (https://pub.dev/packages/shared_preferences) for reading and writing these values in a cross-platform way. Now that you know how to include libraries, it'll be trivial for you to add shared_preferences to your pubspec.yaml file to include it in your project and app.

To use it, you'll need to instantiate a SharedPreferences object. But since we're dealing with reading from the file system, it needs to be handled as a async activity. Fortunately, the library provides a static getInstance() method that returns a Future<SharedPreference>. I know all that sounds confusing, but just remember that getting a reference to the reader/writer is asynchronous. Handle it like this:

```
var prefs = await SharedPreferences.getInstance();
```

See? That's not so bad. But do note that it has to be awaited.

To Write Preferences

To save to shared preferences, use the set methods:

```
prefs
  ..setString('organizationName', organizationName)
  ..setBool('isReady', true)
  ..setDouble('percentComplete', 12.5)
  ..setInt('numberOfTries', tries)
  ..setStringList('validValues', ['started','finished',
                              'in process', 'approved']);
```

Each of these will save to the right incarnation of device-dependent user preferences and return back a Future<bool>, the bool resolving to true if it was successful and false if not. Most developers ignore this value when they're ignoring the extremely rare exception.

To Read Preferences

If writing is with *set* methods, then you'd assume reading is *get* methods and you'd be correct:

```
String? orgName = prefs.getString('organizationName');
bool? isReady = prefs.getBool('isReady');
double? percentComplete = prefs.getDouble('percentComplete');
int? numberOfTries = prefs.getInt('numberOfTries');
List<String>? validValues =prefs.getStringList('validValues');
```

Conclusion

As we said at the top of the appendix, reading and writing files is a complex topic. But what makes it complex is that there are so many technologies and techniques involved: third-party libraries, JSON serialization and deserialization, Futures, and asynchronous reading and writing. All of these topics are covered in this book.

How to Debug Your Layout

As we saw in all of our layout chapters, laying out your screen is pretty darned complicated! Unlike regular imperative code, we can't use a conventional debugger to help us find problems with layout. Fortunately, there is a visual debugger for Flutter. And though it isn't complicated, it does bear some explanation.

Figure E-1 is how your screen might look normally; when you toggle debug painting, you'll see Figure E-2.

R. Payne, *Flutter App Development*, https://doi.org/10.1007/979-8-8688-0485-4

Figure E-1. *Without visual debugging turned on*

Figure E-2. *With visual debugging turned on*

As you can see, it makes your screen suddenly very, very busy! Here's how to decipher what you're seeing:

- All visual boxes get a teal border.

- Padding, margin, and border are colored in blue.

- Alignment/positioning is made obvious with yellow arrows.

- The big green arrows show widgets that can scroll.

- A dashed teal line refers to a boundary imposed by a RenderFlex container. In other words, it shows the constraints of the thing inside it. You may see one of these with a scrolling box like a ListBox or SingleChildScrollView to show the visible portion of that scrolling thing.

Once you get accustomed to them, these visual cues will help you see how Flutter thinks. Understanding the algorithm is key to tuning your layout.

To turn this feature on and off:

- In VS Code, open the command palette (cmd-shift-P or control-shift-P) and type in "Flutter: Toggle debug painting."

- In Android Studio/IntelliJ, go to View ➤ Tool Windows ➤ Flutter Inspector and hit the "Show debug paint" button in the toolbar.

Index

A

AlertDialog, 30, 32, 100, 102
Alignment coordinate system, 233
Alignment numbers, 233
Align widget, 234
analysis_options.yaml, 18
Android emulator, 11–13
Android Studio, 9, 10, 12, 13, 19, 22, 300
Android Virtual Device (AVD) manager, 12, 13
API call, 130
API requests, 131, 132
AppBar widget, 185–186
App's data, 287
Async, 83, 275, 291
Autovalidate, 63
Await, 83, 89, 135, 274–275

B

BlacklistingTextInputFormatter, 55
BLoC pattern, 120–121
Blur radius, 238
BorderOnForeground, 250
BorderRadius, 240–241
BoxConstraints, 192, 193, 236
BoxDecoration, 238, 239

BoxFit options, 47
BoxFit.scaleDown, 46
Box model, 228–231
BoxShadows, 238
BoxShape, 242–244
Brute force, 135–136
Build() method, 33, 35–37, 107, 109, 116, 276, 291
Built-in widgets
    layout widget, 31
    miscellaneous category, 32
    navigation widget, 31
    value widget, 30
Button widgets
    CupertinoButton, 74
    Elevatedbutton, 72
    FloatingActionButton (FAB), 72, 73
    onPressed, 70
    SegmentedButton, 73
    TextButton and IconButton, 72

C

Cascade Operator, 141, 268–269
CHANGELOG.md, 284
Checkboxes widget, 56–57
ColorCircle, 112, 115